OPPOSING VIEWPOINTS® SERIES

| Health

Other Books of Related Interest:

Opposing Viewpoints Series

Organ Donation

At Issue Series

Fast Food

Current Controversies Series

Resistant Infections

"Congress shall make no law . . . abridging the freedom of speech, or of the press."

First Amendment to the U.S. Constitution

The basic foundation of our democracy is the First Amendment guarantee of freedom of expression. The Opposing Viewpoints Series is dedicated to the concept of this basic freedom and the idea that it is more important to practice it than to enshrine it.

OPPOSING VIEWPOINTS® SERIES

Health

Diane Andrews Henningfeld, Book Editor

GREENHAVEN PRESS
A part of Gale, Cengage Learning

Detroit • New York • San Francisco • New Haven, Conn • Waterville, Maine • London

Christine Nasso, *Publisher*
Elizabeth Des Chenes, *Managing Editor*

© 2009 Greenhaven Press, a part of Gale, Cengage Learning.

Gale and Greenhaven Press are registered trademarks used herein under license.

For more information, contact:
Greenhaven Press
27500 Drake Rd.
Farmington Hills, MI 48331-3535
Or you can visit our Internet site at gale.cengage.com

For product information and technology assistance, contact us at

Gale Customer Support, 1-800-877-4253
For permission to use material from this text or product, submit all requests online at www.cengage.com/permissions

Further permissions questions can be emailed to permissionrequest@cengage.com

Articles in Greenhaven Press anthologies are often edited for length to meet page requirements. In addition, original titles of these works are changed to clearly present the main thesis and to explicitly indicate the author's opinion. Every effort is made to ensure that Greenhaven Press accurately reflects the original intent of the authors. Every effort has been made to trace the owners of copyrighted material.

Cover Image copyright Janos Gehring, 2009. Used under license from Shutterstock.com.

LIBRARY OF CONGRESS CATALOGING-IN-PUBLICATION DATA

Health / Diane Andrews Henningfeld, book editor.
    p. cm. -- (Opposing viewpoints)
    Includes bibliographical references and index.
    ISBN 978-0-7377-4520-7 (hardcover)
    ISBN 978-0-7377-4521-4 (pbk.)
    1. Public health. 2. Health. 3. Medical policy. I. Henningfeld, Diane Andrews.
    RA445.H335 2009
    613--dc22

                                        2009016634

20.06   613
          Hea

Printed in the United States of America
1 2 3 4 5 6 7 13 12 11 10 09

Contents

Why Consider Opposing Viewpoints?   11

Introduction   14

Chapter 1: What Are the Greatest Risks to Human Health?

Chapter Preface   19

1. Cancer Rates Are Rising   21
   World Health Organization

2. Cancer Deaths Are Declining   33
   Josephine Marcotty and Richard Meryhew

3. Cardiovascular Disease Kills Humans   39
   *American Heart Association Statistics Committee
   and Stroke Statistics Subcommittee*

4. Cardiovascular Disease Can Be Reduced   44
   Through Lifestyle Changes
   Jeffrey S. Bland

5. Antibiotic Resistant Bacteria Pose a Significant   51
   Threat to Health
   Jerome Groopman

6. Antiobiotic Resistant Infections   59
   Can Be Prevented
   Ridgely Ochs

Periodical Bibliography   65

Chapter 2: What Human Behaviors Contribute to or Damage Health?

Chapter Preface   67

1. Obesity Poses a Serious Health Risk   69
   TeensHealth.org

2. The Health Risks of Obesity Have   77
   Been Exaggerated
   Patrick Basham and Jane Feinman

3. Exercise Can Benefit Health   83
   National Heart, Lung, and Blood Institute

4. Exercise Can Be Harmfully Addictive   90
   Edward J. Cumella

5. Tanning Contributes to Health   97
   The Indoor Tanning Association

6. Tanning Poses Serious Health Risks   102
   Consumers Union of the United States

Periodical Bibliography   110

Chapter 3: Have New Technologies and Treatments Contributed to Human Health?

Chapter Preface   112

1. Statins Can Prevent Cardiovascular Disease   114
   John Carey

2. Statins Pose Serious Health Risks   120
   Byron Richards

3. Osteoporosis Treatments Improve   126
   Women's Health
   Jonathan Labovitz and Shohreh Sayani

4. Osteoporosis Drugs Harm Women's Health   135
   Adriane Fugh-Berman and Charlea T. Massion

5. Health Information Technology Can   141
   Improve Health Care
   Richard Hillestad and James H. Bigelow

6. Health Information Technology Can   148
   Lead to Loss of Patient Privacy
   Deborah C. Peel

Periodical Bibliography   155

Chapter 4: Does America's Health Care System Contribute to Human Health?

Chapter Preface   157

1. America Has the Best Health Care System   160
   in the World
   George W. Bush

2. America Does Not Have the Best Health   168
   Care System in the World
   Ezra Klein

3. A Free-Market Approach to Health Care   176
   Will Keep Costs Down
   Grace-Marie Turner

4. A Free-Market Approach to Health Care   185
   Will Not Lower Health Care Costs
   Uwe E. Reinhardt

Periodical Bibliography   194

For Further Discussion   195

Organizations to Contact   197

Bibliography of Books   202

Index   205

Why Consider Opposing Viewpoints?

> *"The only way in which a human being can make some approach to knowing the whole of a subject is by hearing what can be said about it by persons of every variety of opinion and studying all modes in which it can be looked at by every character of mind. No wise man ever acquired his wisdom in any mode but this."*
>
> John Stuart Mill

In our media-intensive culture it is not difficult to find differing opinions. Thousands of newspapers and magazines and dozens of radio and television talk shows resound with differing points of view. The difficulty lies in deciding which opinion to agree with and which "experts" seem the most credible. The more inundated we become with differing opinions and claims, the more essential it is to hone critical reading and thinking skills to evaluate these ideas. Opposing Viewpoints books address this problem directly by presenting stimulating debates that can be used to enhance and teach these skills. The varied opinions contained in each book examine many different aspects of a single issue. While examining these conveniently edited opposing views, readers can develop critical thinking skills such as the ability to compare and contrast authors' credibility, facts, argumentation styles, use of persuasive techniques, and other stylistic tools. In short, the Opposing Viewpoints Series is an ideal way to attain the higher-level thinking and reading skills so essential in a culture of diverse and contradictory opinions.

In addition to providing a tool for critical thinking, Opposing Viewpoints books challenge readers to question their own strongly held opinions and assumptions. Most people form their opinions on the basis of upbringing, peer pressure, and personal, cultural, or professional bias. By reading carefully balanced opposing views, readers must directly confront new ideas as well as the opinions of those with whom they disagree. This is not to simplistically argue that everyone who reads opposing views will—or should—change his or her opinion. Instead, the series enhances readers' understanding of their own views by encouraging confrontation with opposing ideas. Careful examination of others' views can lead to the readers' understanding of the logical inconsistencies in their own opinions, perspective on why they hold an opinion, and the consideration of the possibility that their opinion requires further evaluation.

Evaluating Other Opinions

To ensure that this type of examination occurs, Opposing Viewpoints books present all types of opinions. Prominent spokespeople on different sides of each issue as well as well-known professionals from many disciplines challenge the reader. An additional goal of the series is to provide a forum for other, less known, or even unpopular viewpoints. The opinion of an ordinary person who has had to make the decision to cut off life support from a terminally ill relative, for example, may be just as valuable and provide just as much insight as a medical ethicist's professional opinion. The editors have two additional purposes in including these less known views. One, the editors encourage readers to respect others' opinions—even when not enhanced by professional credibility. It is only by reading or listening to and objectively evaluating others' ideas that one can determine whether they are worthy of consideration. Two, the inclusion of such viewpoints encourages the important critical thinking skill of objectively evaluating an author's credentials and bias. This evaluation will illuminate an author's reasons for taking a particular stance on an issue and will aid in readers' evaluation of the author's ideas.

It is our hope that these books will give readers a deeper understanding of the issues debated and an appreciation of the complexity of even seemingly simple issues when good and honest people disagree. This awareness is particularly important in a democratic society such as ours in which people enter into public debate to determine the common good. Those with whom one disagrees should not be regarded as enemies but rather as people whose views deserve careful examination and may shed light on one's own.

Thomas Jefferson once said that "difference of opinion leads to inquiry, and inquiry to truth." Jefferson, a broadly educated man, argued that "if a nation expects to be ignorant and free . . . it expects what never was and never will be." As individuals and as a nation, it is imperative that we consider the opinions of others and examine them with skill and discernment. The Opposing Viewpoints Series is intended to help readers achieve this goal.

David L. Bender and Bruno Leone,
Founders

Introduction

> "Older adults are more likely to suffer chronic illnesses (cancer, heart disease, diabetes) and need more and different health services than younger adults. Yet, most health professionals receive limited training on care to older adults and, in future, will need better training in geriatric issues, such as chronic disease management."
>
> *Catherine Herman*

Between 1946 and 1964, the United States experienced what has come to be known as the post-World War II "baby boom." During those years, birth rates went up dramatically. As a result, American society has had to accommodate a large number of similarly aged people through each stage of their development. For example, the first baby boomers reached school age in about 1952. With each successive year, more and more baby boomers entered elementary school. This meant that many communities had to build more schools and facilities to accommodate the number of children eligible for public education. Baby boomers experienced crowded classrooms and teacher shortages, among other conditions, caused by their sheer numbers.

In the first decade of the twenty-first century, the oldest of the baby boomers are entering what has traditionally been considered old age. According to a 2006 report from the Federal Interagency Forum on Aging, "The Baby Boomers . . . will start turning 65 in 2011, and the numbers of older people will increase dramatically during the 2010–2030 period. The older population is projected to be twice as large as in 2000, growing from 35 million to 71.5 million and representing nearly 20 percent of the total U.S. population." Data released from the U.S. Census Bureau in May 2008 in recognition of Older Americans Month reveals that in 2050, the projected population of people older than 65 will reach 86.7 million, or 21 percent of the total U.S. population.

Just as the baby boomers placed unprecedented pressure on social and educational infrastructures in the 1960s and 1970s, they will dramatically affect health and health care in the United States during the first half of the twenty-first century. One result of the growth of the older population will be an increase in chronic diseases often associated with the elderly, including a variety of cancers, heart disease, and diabetes. According to Robert Preidt, writing in *HealthDay News* on February 25, 2008, "While the number of elderly Americans newly diagnosed with heart failure has declined, the number of those living with the condition has increased. . . . Since it's primarily a disease of older people, it places a significant and increasing burden on Medicare." Preidt further cites a study from the *Archives of Internal Medicine* that demonstrates a 30 percent increase in the number of people 65 and older hospitalized for heart failure between 1984 and 2002. This number is likely to increase with the growing number of elderly people in the population.

Prostate cancer will also likely increase as the population ages. The Prostate Cancer Foundation reveals that although only 1 in 10,000 men under age 40 are diagnosed with prostate cancer, the rate is 1 in 15 for men 65 to 69 years old. The foundation further notes that more than 65 percent of all prostate cancers are diagnosed in men over the age of 65. Because prostate cancer is a slow-growing cancer, many men will need treatment for the disease as they grow older.

For women, one of the greatest risks to health and vitality is osteoporosis, the gradual thinning of the bones that accelerates once a woman reaches menopause. Although osteoporosis does not by itself cause death, it leads to serious and severe bone fractures that often disable older women, since fractures heal much more slowly with advancing age. Indeed, many women suffer from debilitating spinal compression fractures that cause extreme pain and incapacity. According to Jay Herson in his article "The Coming Osteoporosis Epidemic," "In the United States, about 10 million people have osteoporosis, and 34 million have osteopenia [below-average bone mineral density]. These numbers are expected to increase to 14 and 47 million, respectively, by 2020." Because of this increase, demand for home health care aides will also increase in the future as female baby boomers feel the full effects of osteoporosis.

The incidence of Alzheimer's disease also increases with age. The *2008 Alzheimer's Disease Facts and Figures*, published by the Alzheimer's Association projects that 10 million baby boomers will suffer from Alzheimer's. The biggest risk factor for Alzheimer's is age; nearly all cases occur in people over 65. Among people 85 years old or older, 50 percent will have Alzheimer's. Already the sixth leading cause of death in the United States, Alzheimer's imposes a burden on patients, and their families, that will dramatically increase as the population ages.

Finally, the aging population will also tax health care in the United States due to accidents. Older drivers tend to die or suffer severe injuries in car accidents more frequently than do younger drivers, according to a study reported in the January 5, 2007, issue of *Senior Journal.com*. People injured in such accidents often require significant hospital stays and medical care.

It is likely that just as baby boomers faced shortages in classroom space in the 1950s and 1960s, they will also face room shortages in assisted living facilities and nursing homes in the twenty-first century. Likewise, the numbers of younger people who will be required to offer care to the elderly will greatly increase, and it is likely that the health care industry will have severe shortages in gerontologists, geriatric nurses, and home health care aids. As more baby boomers retire, fewer dollars will flow into Medicare, the primary health insurance for Americans over the age of 65; at the same time, as baby boomers age, they will draw more heavily on medical services, drawing more dollars out of the Medicare system.

The effects of the baby boom on American health, among both the young and old, will continue to manifest themselves over the next forty to fifty years. Only through new technologies, new treatments, and new ways of thinking about health care resources will America successfully accommodate the aging population. In the following chapters, "What Are the Greatest Risks to Human Health?", "What Human Behaviors Contribute to or Damage Health?", "Have New Technologies and Treatments Contributed to Human Health?", and "Does America's Health Care System Contribute to Human Health?", writers tackle some of the thorniest issues concerning health and wellness in the United States. Their viewpoints offer multiple perspectives on very real problems.

CHAPTER 1

What Are the Greatest Risks to Human Health?

Chapter Preface

If asked to consider the greatest risks to human health, people might immediately name diseases such as cancer, heart disease, and AIDS at the top of their lists. Likewise, obesity, drug addiction, tobacco use, and alcoholism also represent serious threats to human health. Climate change, on the other hand, might not even come to mind as a serious health risk; however, according to scientists, epidemiologists, geographers, and sociologists, climate change will seriously affect human health for years, even centuries, to come. As the Secretariat of the World Health Organization noted in 2008, "Climate change will affect, in profoundly adverse ways, some of the most fundamental determinants of health: food, air, and water."

The most obvious connection between climate change and health is the increasing number of deadly heat waves across the globe. Not only do people die when they are unable to cool themselves adequately, but heat waves also cause drought conditions that kill crops. Inadequate nutrition, caused by drought and famine, renders people more vulnerable to a host of infectious diseases. Likewise, high temperatures and drought cause wildfires that destroy property, kill people, and cause smoke-induced illness and injury.

Moreover, as the Secretariat of the World Health Organization further argued, "Global warming is expected to pose direct threats to health by causing more severe storms, floods, droughts and fires with consequent disruptions in water and food supplies and medical and other services." Hurricanes, such as the one that struck Myanmar (Burma) in May 2008, leaving as many as 100,000 dead or missing, and Katrina, which struck the Gulf Coast of the United States in 2005, are predicted to become more frequent and more devastating. In addition to the initial death tolls of such storms, disruptions in water sanitation and food distribution will add additional health risks.

Scientists also agree that an increase in average temperatures world wide will increase the incidence of food- and water-borne infectious diseases, such as cholera. Further, a warmer climate worldwide will extend the range of malaria-carrying mosquitoes into areas where malaria has not previously been a problem, including regions of the southern United States. Diseases caused by fungi, mold, and rot will also affect livestock and crops throughout the world, further threatening food supplies and human health.

As humans attempt to cope with rising temperatures, they will impose further demands on energy sources to provide cooling and irrigation for people, animals, and crops. This demand in turn may cause additional burning of fossil fuels, which can exacerbate the problems. In terms of human health, an increase in energy production can lead to a decrease in air quality. A major concern for the Chinese government during the 2008 Beijing Olympics, for example, was the degradation of air quality caused by coal-burning plants throughout the country. Such degradation causes increases in respiratory diseases and the incidence of asthma.

Although people are now living longer and healthier lives than has been the case throughout much of history, there are still serious threats to human health, as documented by the writers of the viewpoints in this chapter. Many people believe that, among those threats, climate change may prove to be the most serious.

> "The predicted sharp increase in new cases ... will mainly be due to steadily ageing populations in both developed and developing countries and also to current trends in smoking prevalence and the growing adoption of unhealthy lifestyles."

Cancer Rates Are Rising

World Health Organization

In the following viewpoint, the World Health Organization (WHO) asserts that cancer rates could dramatically increase around the world and that cancer is a major health problem worldwide. Tobacco is cited as a potent risk factor for cancer. The WHO further argues that although cancer has traditionally been a disease of developed nations, as developing nations adopt Western lifestyles, including increased smoking and diets high in fats, protein, and calories, their cancer rates are rising sharply. The World Health Organization is an arm of the United Nations responsible for coordinating international health activities.

World Health Organization, "Global Cancer Rates Could Increase 50% to 15 Million by 2020," World Health Organization: Media Center, April 3, 2003. © WHO 2003. Reproduced by permission.

As you read, consider the following questions:

1. According to the WHO, how many people worldwide died from tobacco-associated diseases in the twentieth century?

2. What percentage of malignancies are caused by infectious agents in developing countries?

3. Which of the industrial nations have the highest overall cancer rates?

Cancer rates could further increase by 50% to 15 million new cases in the year 2020, according to the *World Cancer Report*, the most comprehensive global examination of the disease to date. However, the report also provides clear evidence that healthy lifestyles and public health action by governments and health practitioners could stem this trend, and prevent as many as one third of cancers worldwide.

Cancer Is a Major Health Problem

In the year 2000, malignant tumours were responsible for 12 per cent of the nearly 56 million deaths worldwide from all causes. In many countries, more than a quarter of deaths are attributable to cancer. In 2000, 5.3 million men and 4.7 million women developed a malignant tumour and altogether 6.2 million died from the disease. The report also reveals that cancer has emerged as a major public health problem in developing countries, matching its effect in industrialized nations.

"The *World Cancer Report* tells us that cancer rates are set to increase at an alarming rate globally. We can make a difference by taking action today. We have the opportunity to stem this increase. This report calls on Governments, health practitioners and the general public to take urgent action. Action now can prevent one third of cancers, cure another third, and provide good, palliative care to the remaining third who need it," said Dr. Paul Kleihues, Director of the International Agency for Research on Cancer (IARC) and co-editor of the *World Cancer Report*. . . .

Examples of areas where action can make a difference to stemming the increase of cancer rates and preventing a third of cases are:

- Reduction of tobacco consumption. It remains the most important avoidable cancer risk. In the 20th century, approximately 100 million people died world-wide from tobacco-associated diseases.

- A healthy lifestyle and diet can help. Frequent consumption of fruit and vegetables and physical activity can make a difference.

- Early detection through screening, particularly for cervical and breast cancers, allows for prevention and successful cure.

The predicted sharp increase in new cases—from 10 million new cases globally in 2000, to 15 million in 2020—will mainly be due to steadily ageing populations in both developed and developing countries and also to current trends in smoking prevalence and the growing adoption of unhealthy lifestyles.

"Governments, physicians, and health educators at all levels could do much more to help people change their behaviour to avoid preventable cancers," says Bernard W. Stewart, Ph.D., co-editor of the report, Director of Cancer Services, and Professor, Faculty of Medicine, University of New South Wales, Australia. "If the knowledge, technology and control strategies outlined in the *World Cancer Report* were applied globally, we would make major advances in preventing and treating cancers over the next twenty years and beyond."

"From a global perspective, there is strong justification for focusing cancer prevention activities particularly on two main cancer-causing factors—tobacco and diet. We also need to continue efforts to curb infections which cause cancers," said Dr Rafael Bengoa, Director, Management of Non-communicable disease at WHO [World Health Organization]. "These factors were responsible for 43 per cent of all cancer deaths in 2000, that is 2.7 million fatalities, and 40 per cent of all new cases, that is four million new cancer cases." . . .

Tobacco Greatly Increases the Risk of Cancer

Tobacco consumption remains the most important avoidable cancer risk. In the 20th century, approximately 100 million people died worldwide from tobacco-associated diseases (cancer, chronic lung disease, cardiovascular disease and stroke). Half of regular smokers are killed by the habit. One quarter of smokers will die prematurely during middle age (35 to 69 years).

The lung cancer risk for regular smokers as compared to non-smokers (relative risk, RR) is between 20 and 30 fold. In countries with a high smoking prevalence and where many women have smoked cigarettes throughout adult life, roughly 90 per cent of lung cancers in both men and women are attributable to cigarette smoking. For bladder and renal pelvis, the RR is five-six, but this means that more than 50 per cent of cases are caused by smoking.

The RR for cancers of the oral cavity . . . pharynx, larynx and squamous cell carcinoma of the oesophagus is greater than six, and three-four for carcinomas of the pancreas. These risk estimates are higher than previously estimated, and unfortunately, additional cancer sites with a RR of two-three have been identified as being associated with tobacco smoking, including cancers of the stomach, liver, uterine cervix, kidney (renal cell carcinoma), nasal cavities and sinuses, esophagus (adenocarcinoma) and myeloid leukaemia.

Involuntary (passive) tobacco smoke is carcinogenic and may increase the lung cancer risk by 20 per cent. There is currently no evidence that smoking causes breast, prostate or endometrial cancer of the uterus.

The deadly smoking habit is particularly worrying in Central and Eastern Europe and many developing and newly industrialized countries. The tendency of youth around the world to start smoking at younger and younger ages will predispose them to substantial risks in later life.

While it is best never to start smoking, epidemiological evidence supports the enormous benefits of cessation. The greatest reduction in the number of cancer deaths within the next several decades will be due to those who stop the habit. The greatest effect results from stopping smoking in the early 30s, but a very impressive risk reduction of more than 60 per cent is obtained even when the habit is quit after the age of 50 years. . . .

The Cancer-Infection Connection

In developing countries, up to 23 per cent of malignancies are caused by infectious agents, including hepatitis B [HBV] and C virus (liver cancer), human papillomaviruses (cervical and ano-genital cancers), and Helicobacter pylori (stomach cancer). In developed countries, cancers caused by chronic infections only amount to approximately 8 per cent of all malignancies. This discrepancy is particularly evident for cervical cancer. In developed countries with an excellent public health infrastructure and a high compliance of women, early cytological detection of cervical cancer (PAP smear) has led to an impressive reduction of mortality, while in other world regions, including Central America, South East Africa and India, incidence and mortality rates are still very high. Today, more than 80 per cent of all cervical cancer deaths occur in developing countries.

The Leading Cancer Types for Estimated New Cancers and Deaths, 2008

Estimated New Cases in the United States

Males			Females		
Prostate	186,320	25%	Breast	182,460	26%
Lung & bronchus	114,690	15%	Lung & bronchus	100,330	14%
Colon & rectum	77,250	10%	Colon & rectum	71,560	10%
Urinary bladder	51,230	7%	Uterine corpus	40,100	6%
Non-Hodgkins lymphoma	35,450	5%	Non-Hodgkins lymphoma	30,670	4%
Melanoma of the skin	34,950	5%	Thyroid	28,410	4%
Kidney & renal pelvis	33,130	4%	Melanoma of the skin	27,530	4%
Oral cavity & pharynx	25,310	3%	Ovary	21,650	3%
Leukemia	25,180	3%	Kidney & renal pelvis	21,260	3%
Pancreas	18,770	3%	Leukemia	19,090	3%
All sites	745,180	100%	All sites	692,000	100%

[CONTINUED]

The Leading Cancer Types for Estimated New Cancers and Deaths, 2008 [CONTINUED]

Estimated Deaths in the United States

	Males			Females	
Lung & bronchus	90,810	31%	Lung & bronchus	71,030	26%
Prostate	28,660	10%	Breast	40,480	15%
Colon & rectum	24,260	8%	Colon & rectum	25,700	9%
Pancreas	17,500	6%	Pancreas	16,790	6%
Liver & intrahepatic bile duct	12,570	4%	Ovary	15,520	6%
Leukemia	12,460	4%	Non-Hodgkins lymphoma	9,370	3%
Esophagus	11,250	4%	Leukemia	9,250	3%
Urinary bladder	9,950	3%	Uterine corpus	7,470	3%
Non-Hodgkins lymphoma	9,790	3%	Liver & intrahepatic bile duct	5,840	2%
Kidney & renal pelvis	8,100	3%	Brain & other nervous system	5,650	2%
All sites	**294,120**	**100%**	**All sites**	**271,530**	**100%**

TAKEN FROM: "Cancer Statistics, 2008," *CA: A Cancer Journal for Clinicians*, October 14, 2008. caonline.amcancersoc.org.

Vaccinations could be key to preventing these cancers. HBV vaccination has already been shown to prevent liver cancer in high-incidence countries and it is likely that human papillomavirus (HPV) vaccination will become a reality in 3 to 5 years.

In the gastro-intestinal tract (GIT), any chronic tissue damage with necrosis and regeneration carries an increased cancer risk, e.g. consumption of very hot beverages (squamous cell carcinoma of the esophagus), gastro-oesophageal reflux (adenocarcinoma of the esophagus), chronic gastritis induced by H. pylori infection (stomach cancer), Crohn's disease (cancer of the small intestines) and ulcerative colitis (colon cancer). . . .

In developed countries, the probability of being diagnosed with cancer is more than twice as high as in developing countries. However, in rich countries, some 50 per cent of cancer patients die of the disease, while in developing countries, 80 per cent of cancer victims already have late-stage incurable tumors when they are diagnosed, pointing to the need for much better detection programs.

The main reasons for the greater cancer burden of affluent societies are the earlier onset of the tobacco epidemic, the earlier exposure to occupational carcinogens, and the Western nutrition and lifestyle. However, with increasing wealth and industrialization, many countries undergo rapid lifestyle changes that will greatly increase their future disease burden.

Once considered a "Western" disease, the *Report* highlights that more than 50 per cent of the world's cancer burden, in terms of both numbers of cases and deaths, already occurs in developing countries. "Cancer has emerged as a major public health problem in developing countries for the first time, matching its effect in industrialized nations. This is a global problem, and it's growing. But, we can take steps to slow this growth," says Paul Kleihues, MD, Director of IARC and co-editor of the *World Cancer Report*.

The Western Lifestyle Contributes to Increasing Cancer Rates

The Western lifestyle is characterized by a highly caloric diet, rich in fat, refined carbohydrates and animal protein, combined with low physical activity, resulting in an overall energy imbalance. It is associated with a multitude of disease conditions, including obesity, diabetes, cardiovascular disease, arterial hypertension and cancer.

Malignancies typical for affluent societies are cancers of the breast, colon/rectum, uterus (endometrial carcinoma), gallbladder, kidney and adenocarcinoma of the oesophagus. Prostate cancer is also strongly related to the Western lifestyle, but there is an additional ethnic component; black people appear to be at a greater risk than whites and the latter at higher risk than Asian populations. Similar lifestyles are associated with a similar tumour burden. Since they have a common cause, these neoplasms typically go together. There is no region in the world that has a high incidence of breast cancer without a concurrent colon cancer burden.

Obesity is spreading epidemically throughout the world. It visualizes a chronic energy imbalance and is an independent predictor of an increased cancer risk, particularly for carcinomas of the uterine endometrium, kidney and gall bladder.

Stomach cancer is among the most common malignancies worldwide, with some 870,000 cases every year, and 650,000 deaths. About 60 per cent of cases occur in developing countries, with the highest incidence rates coming in Eastern Asia, the Andean regions of South America and Eastern Europe. The good news is that stomach cancer is declining worldwide, in some regions almost dramatically. In Switzerland and neighbouring European countries, the mortality fell by 60 per cent within one generation. If this trend continues, stomach cancer may in some world regions become a rare disease during the next 30 years. The main reason for this welcome development is the invention of the refrigerator, allowing fish and meat preservation without salting. The drop in incidence and mortality rates is therefore particularly impressive in Nordic countries in which fish consumption is traditionally high, e.g. Iceland. In populations that still prefer salty food, e.g. Portugal and Brazil (salted cod, bacalao), Japan and Korea (salted pickles and salad), stomach cancer rates are still high but have also started to decline significantly. An additional factor contributing to this trend is the availability in many countries of fresh fruit and vegetables throughout the year.

A Healthy Diet Protects People from Cancer

Epidemiological studies indicate that the frequent consumption of fruit and vegetables may reduce the risk of developing cancers of epithelial origin, including carcinomas of the pharynx, larynx, lung, oesophagus, stomach, colon and cervix. Recent data from the European Prospective Investigation into Cancer and Nutrition (EPIC), suggests that a daily consumption of 500 grams (1.1. lbs.) of fruits and vegetables can decrease incidence of cancers of the digestive tract by up to 25 per cent.

The report also says that given the multi-faceted impact of diet on cancer, many countries should encourage consumption of locally produced vegetables, fruit and agricultural products, and avoid the adoption of Western style dietary habits. IARC says that such actions would have health benefits beyond cancer, since other common non-communicable diseases, notably cardiovascular disease and diabetes, share the same lifestyle-related risk factors.

Early detection [is] the best strategy second to primary prevention. The best possible prevention against cancer remains the avoidance of exposure to cancer-causing agents: this is called primary prevention (eg tobacco, industrial carcinogens, etc). . . .

The Most Common and Most Deadly Cancers

Lung cancer is the most common cancer worldwide, accounting for 1.2 million new cases annually; followed by cancer of the breast, just over 1 million cases; colorectal, 940,000; stomach, 870,000; liver, 560,000; cervical, 470,000, esophageal, 410,000; head and neck, 390,000; bladder, 330,000; malignant non-Hodgkin lymphomas, 290,000; leukemia, 250,000; prostate and testicular, 250,000; pancreatic, 216,000; ovarian, 190,000; kidney, 190,000; endometrial, 188,000; nervous system, 175,000; melanoma, 133,000; thyroid, 123,000; pharynx, 65,000; and Hodgkin disease, 62,000 cases.

The three leading cancer killers are different than the three most common forms, with lung cancer responsible for 17.8 per cent of all cancer deaths, stomach, 10.4 per cent and liver, 8.8 per cent.

Industrial nations with the highest overall cancer rates include: U.S.A., Italy, Australia, Germany, The Netherlands, Canada and France. Developing countries with the lowest cancer were in Northern Africa, Southern and Eastern Asia. . . .

Lung cancer strikes 900,000 men and 330,000 women yearly. Among men, smoking causes more than 80 per cent of lung cancer cases. In women, smoking is the cause of 45 per cent of all lung cancer worldwide, but more than 70 per cent in North America and Northern Europe. In both men and women, the incidence of lung cancer is low before age 40, and increases up to age 70 or 75.

The rise in female smoking prevalence is a major public health concern. In the US, more women die from smoking-induced lung cancer than from breast cancer and in some Nordic countries, including Iceland and Denmark, female lung cancer deaths have begun to outnumber male tobacco victims. Considering that in several European countries up to 50 per cent of young women are now regular smokers, this will cause a disease burden that significantly reduces women's health in decades to come. . . .

Cancers of the colon and rectum are rare in developing countries, but are the second most frequent malignancy in affluent societies. More than 940,000 cases occur annually worldwide, and nearly 500,000 die from it each year.

A major cause is a diet rich in fat, refined carbohydrates and animal protein, combined with low physical activity. Genetic susceptibility appears to be involved in less than five per cent of cases. Epidemiological studies suggest that risk can be reduced by decreasing meat consumption (particularly processed meat) and increasing the intake of vegetables and fruit. Migrant populations rapidly reach the higher level of risk of the adopted country, another sign that environmental factors play a major role.

Colonoscopy is the most reliable means for early detection. Progressively improved diagnosis and treatment has resulted in a five-year survival rate of 50 per cent.

> *"A nationwide decrease of 369 [cancer] deaths reported for 2003, the first in more than 70 years, appears to be the start of a sustained decline."*

Cancer Deaths Are Declining

Josephine Marcotty and Richard Meryhew

In the following viewpoint, journalists Josephine Marcotty and Richard Meryhew report that cancer deaths are dropping nationwide, according to 2007 data from the American Cancer Society. Minnesota, in particular, showed a marked decline in cancer deaths. The writers argue that this is due to Minnesotans undergoing screening tests leading to early detection. New treatments are also helping cancer victims live longer, assert the writers. Marcotty and Meryhew write for the Minneapolis Star Tribune.

As you read, consider the following questions:

1. What cancer showed the greatest decline in mortality in 2004, according to the viewpoint?

2. In what year did the actual number of deaths from cancer drop enough to outpace aging and population growth?

3. What population in the United States shows a considerably higher cancer death rate for nearly every type of cancer?

The war against cancer is far from over, but it may have reached a turning point. Cancer deaths dropped in 2004 for the second year in a row, a decline even more pronounced in Minnesota than for the country as a whole. A new report from the American Cancer Society shows that a nationwide decrease of 369 deaths reported for 2003, the first in more than 70 years, appears to be the start of a sustained decline rather than a statistical fluke, the society said. The trend accelerated in 2004, when cancer deaths fell by 3,014, or 0.5 percent.

In Minnesota, there were 9,091 cancer deaths in 2004, 1 percent less than the previous year.

"What appears to be a sustained trend is very gratifying," said Dr. Mark Wilkowske, chief of oncology services at Park Nicollet Cancer Center. "The sky is the limit for the future."

The Change Is Caused by Better Detection and Treatment

Much of the change was attributed to smoking cessation and better detection and treatment of three of the most common cancers—colorectal, breast and prostate, the American Cancer Society said. Cancer is the second leading cause of death in the United States, after heart disease.

By far, the greatest U.S. decrease in mortality in 2004 was in colon cancer, with 1,110 fewer deaths in men and 1,094 fewer in women. In fact, Minnesota owes its larger overall decline in cancer deaths entirely to its proportionately larger decrease in deaths from colon cancer. There were more than 150 fewer such deaths in 2004 than 2003, said Matt Flory, health promotions director for the American Cancer Society in Minnesota.

That's because Minnesotans are better than just about anyone else in stepping up for colon screening tests. The screening methods include stool tests; colonoscopy, which examines the entire large intestine; and sigmoidoscopy, which examines the lower part of it.

Flory said that 60 percent of the people in this state who should have colonoscopies get them. That's a far higher rate than most other states and the national average of about 50 percent, he said. Doctors and cancer survivors said the numbers are proof the advanced research and treatments they've been seeing for the past several years are working. "It's interesting to watch where these doctors' and researchers' minds are going," said Laurie Whitt, 45, of Maple Grove, who was diagnosed with breast cancer 11 years ago. "They are thinking outside the box, which is so cool." . . .

Although the drop in deaths is noteworthy, it still pales in comparison to the total of 553,888 cancer deaths in 2004. The death rate from cancer has been falling by slightly less than 1 percent a year since 1991. But until 2003 the actual number of deaths kept rising because the population was growing and aging.

That year, the cumulative drop in death rates finally became large enough to outpace aging and population growth.

New Treatments Are Extending Lives

"I wasn't sure it would happen in my lifetime," said Tim Church, an expert on prevention and early detection of cancer at the University of Minnesota. Experts said that in addition to better early detection through screening, new drugs and treatments have extended lives of people who would have died much sooner. "There was a revolution in treatment between 1998 and 2000, and revolution is a mild word," said Dr. Alfred Neugut, head of cancer prevention and control at Columbia University Medical Center. "We went from having one drug to having six or seven good drugs. The cure and survival rates have increased dramatically as a result."

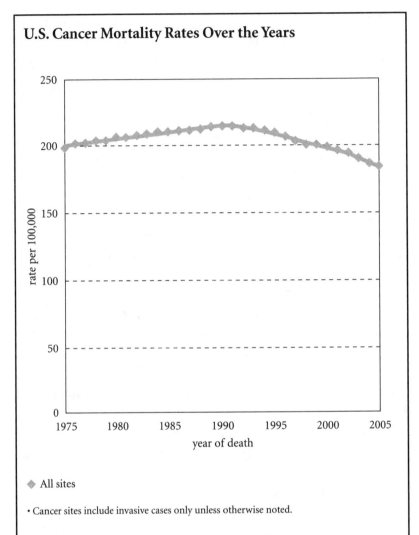

U.S. Cancer Mortality Rates Over the Years

◆ All sites

• Cancer sites include invasive cases only unless otherwise noted.

TAKEN FROM: US Mortality Files, National Center for Health Statistics, CDC. Rates are per 100,000 and are age-adjusted to the 2000 US Std Population (19 age groups-Census P25-1130). Regression lines are calculated using the Joinpoint Regression Program Version 3.3, April 2008, National Cancer Institute.

And colorectal screening, Neuget said, was comparable to the Pap test, which led to an 85 percent decrease in cervical cancer cases in this country.

"It's a whole different ballgame for a cancer survivor now," said Pat Harwood, 54, of St. Louis Park, who was diagnosed with stage 3 multiple myeloma, a cancer of the bone marrow, in 1996. "Every year you live could be a lifetime because of the new research coming on the market." Ruth Edstrom, 58, of Minneapolis, credits a colonoscopy in late 1999 with helping to save her life.

Although she had experienced symptoms of colon cancer for several years, she said the disease wasn't detected until a doctor performed a colonoscopy. By the time cancer was spotted, it had spread to her liver. But she had several successful surgeries and six months of chemotherapy. She is cancer free today, and so are her younger siblings. After her experience, she persuaded all four to have colonoscopies. The screening paid off—doctors spotted and removed a precancerous polyp from the colon of her brother.

"Go out and get yourself checked," said Whitt, of Maple Grove. "Go in and get a mammogram. Go get a colonoscopy. We all have to be on top of our game at all times. We cannot let our guard down. Something could sneak up."

African Americans Have Higher Rates of Cancer Deaths

The American Cancer Society said it expects that deaths will continue to decline, and other experts agreed. Church said that there are large studies now underway to test the effectiveness of screening for lung cancer, still the leading cause of cancer deaths. There are also major studies underway to test the effectiveness of advance screening tests for prostate cancer, he said. One area of great concern, said Dr. Elizabeth Ward, the cancer society's managing director in epidemiology and surveillance, are the considerably higher cancer death rates among African Americans for nearly every type of cancer. Researchers do not fully understand why. Disparities in income, education and access to health care could account for much of the difference, but not all of it, researchers say.

"If we really want to continue to make progress by applying what we know," Ward said, "we have to figure out a way to make sure to reach all populations with the information they need to prevent cancer and make sure that all populations have access to early detection and treatment—quality treatment—so that 10 to 20 years from now we don't see the same big differences."

"Heart and blood vessel diseases remain major public health problems for men and women of all races in the United States, and are costly in terms of human life and in dollars."

Cardiovascular Disease Kills Humans

American Heart Association Statistics Committee and Stroke Statistics Subcommittee

In the following viewpoint, the authors argue that although cardiovascular disease death rates are going down, it remains the leading cause of death among both men and women in the United States. In addition, the authors assert, because risk factors for heart and blood vessel diseases are rising due to increased smoking and obesity, more people will require treatment for cardiovascular disease at a very high cost. The American Heart Association is a national, volunteer health organization whose mission statement is "Building healthier lives, free of cardiovascular diseases and stroke."

As you read, consider the following questions:

1. In what year in the twentieth century was cardiovascular disease *not* the leading cause of death since 1900?

2. How many United States teenagers try smoking every day, according to the American Heart Association?

3. How much did experts estimate the costs of treating cardiovascular disease in 2008 would be?

Cardiovascular disease death rates are going down but it remains the major cause of death in the United States. In 2004, the most recent year for which final statistics were available, there was an overall age-adjusted (AA) death rate of 288 per 100,000 people. Controlling cardiovascular disease risk factors still remains a challenge.

Understanding heart disease and how effective efforts are to reduce it is important to future public health efforts. Understanding what problems remain can help policymakers determine where to direct their efforts to reduce heart disease and stroke.

What We Know About Heart Disease

Coronary heart disease, stroke, high blood pressure, heart failure and all other heart- and blood vessel-related problems have been the major cause of death in the United States every year since 1900 except during the 1918 flu pandemic. Several risk factors contribute to heart disease, including high blood pressure, high blood cholesterol levels, and type 2 diabetes. Common U.S. lifestyle habits—including high-fat, high-salt diets and low levels of physical activity—contribute to obesity and overweight, both of which are related to heart disease. Those with cardiovascular risk factors such as hypertension and diabetes also have more kidney disease which cause the kidneys to no longer function normally.

Each year, the American Heart Association, along with the Centers for Disease Control and Prevention, the National Institutes of Health and other government agencies, pool their information to provide the public and health professionals with the most current statistics on heart disease, stroke and their risk factors.

The overall AA death rate from cardiovascular disease remains high [in 2007] at 288 deaths per 100,000 people, but it represents a decrease from an AA rate of 307.7 deaths per 100,000 recorded in 2003. In total, cardiovascular disease accounted for 869,724 deaths in 2004 compared to 911,163 deaths in 2003. Stroke was the No. 3 U.S. killer, responsible for 150,074 deaths. Coronary heart disease accounted for 451,326 deaths—making it (still) the single No. 1 killer in the nation.

"These statistics make it clear that cardiovascular disease remains, by far, our greatest public health challenge," said Donald Lloyd-Jones, M.D., Sc.M., chair of the association's Statistics Committee, which, along with the association's Stroke Statistics Subcommittee, is responsible for the Update, in a released statement. Lloyd-Jones is also an associate professor in the Department of Preventive Medicine at Northwestern University's Feinberg School of Medicine in Chicago. "Although we have made some substantial strides in understanding the causes of cardiovascular disease, the data in this publication show that we have a long way to go to capture people's attention and to implement the prevention and treatment programs we need."

Risk Factors Are High

Lloyd-Jones and colleagues pointed out that while death rates from heart and blood vessel disease appear to be dropping, many risk factors remain at high levels or are even increasing. The rate of overweight in adults and children continues to rise, with 66 percent of U.S. adults classified as overweight and 31.4 percent as obese. Among U.S. children and teens, 17 percent are overweight.

Heart Disease Statistics and Facts

- Heart disease is the number one killer of women in the United States.

- In a 2003, survey, only 13% of women perceived heart disease as their greatest health problem.

- Heart disease is the number one killer of men in the United States.

- Men have a 49% lifetime risk of developing coronary heart disease after the age of 40.

- Worldwide, heart disease kills more than 7 million people each year.

- Major risk factors for heart disease include high blood pressure, tobacco use, diabetes, high blood cholesterol, poor nutrition, and physical inactivity.

- The average age of a first heart attack for men is 66.

- Nearly 50% of all men who have a heart attack under age 65 die within 8 years.

Centers for Disease Control and Prevention, 2008, www.cdc.gov.

In addition, more than 46 million U.S. adults smoke cigarettes daily and 4,000 U.S. teens try smoking every day. Diabetes, another risk factor for heart disease, continues to grow, with estimates that its prevalence will double between 2005 and 2050. Currently, an estimated 15.1 million people have physician-diagnosed diabetes and another 6 million have undiagnosed diabetes and one-third are unaware of it. Another 59.7 million people have levels of glucose circulating in their blood which are higher than normal but under the threshold of the levels in people with diabetes, a condition called pre-diabetes which greatly increases the risk of diabetes. Chronic kidney disease and end-stage renal disease are also increasing; it is projected that the number of people requiring treatment for kidney failure will increase 60 percent between 2001 and 2010.

The Cost of Care

Care for people with cardiovascular disease is improving, particularly for heart disease, with many patients receiving the recommended treatments. At the same time, the cost of such care is also climbing. Experts estimate that the costs of treating cardiovascular disease will rise to $448.5 billion in 2008, over $16 billion more than in 2007.

Death rates for heart disease in the United States are dropping but the presence of risk factors for developing heart disease are unchanged or increasing. Find out your risks for heart disease. If you already have heart disease, follow your physician's instructions for managing your disease. Heart and blood vessel diseases remain major public health problems for men and women of all races in the United States, and are costly in terms of human life and in dollars. Reducing these diseases requires major intervention at both the public health and personal level. Talk to your doctor to find out what you can do to reduce your own risk as well as that of your family and friends.

"Wide-scale savings (billions of dollars and, more importantly, hundreds of thousands of lives) derived from therapeutic lifestyle changes (TLC) have been amply demonstrated."

Cardiovascular Disease Can Be Reduced Through Lifestyle Changes

Jeffrey S. Bland

In the following viewpoint, Jeffrey S. Bland asserts that the number of people suffering from chronic diseases, including cardiovascular disease, could be greatly reduced through simple lifestyle changes such as moderate exercise and weight loss. This would, he argues, reduce health care costs dramatically as well as save lives. Bland advises health care providers to incorporate therapeutic lifestyle changes into their practices. Bland is a nutritional biochemist and the author of several books on nutritional medicine.

As you read, consider the following questions:

1. In the United States, how much money is spent annually on the diagnosis and treatment of chronic illnesses, according to Bland?

2. What health benefits are realized through a sustained 10 percent weight loss, according to Bland?

3. What allied health professionals ought to be included in a TLC team, according to Bland?

You see them every day: patients with, or at risk of developing, lifestyle-related chronic diseases. In the United States, type 2 diabetes, cardiovascular disease and other chronic conditions have reached epidemic proportions, affecting nearly half of the population and contributing to seven of every 10 deaths.

Perhaps even more disturbing is that these numbers could be drastically reduced with widespread adoption of simple lifestyle changes, including healthier eating and moderate exercise. Yet despite overwhelming clinical and scientific evidence, most health care practitioners fail to counsel their patients on these important issues.

In the U.S., one in three adults is obese. One in five children is overweight and likely to carry their health-related problems into adulthood. Twenty-one million people have diabetes, including 6 million who don't know they have it. Another 54 million are insulin-resistant. One in five adults has doctor-diagnosed arthritis.

Similar numbers have been reported from all seven continents. According to the World Health Organization, lifestyle-related chronic diseases contribute to 60 percent of all deaths and 80 percent of deaths in low- and middle-income countries.

The High Cost of Disease

In the U.S., more than $1.5 trillion is spent annually on the diagnosis and treatment of chronic illnesses, including $60 billion for five of the top 10 classes of blockbuster drugs. How are we spending so much and getting so little in return? It's worth noting that the American health-care delivery and financial-reimbursement systems traditionally have been structured on the use of high-cost diagnostics, procedures and pharmaceuticals developed to treat acute illness, while less emphasis has been placed on wellness and prevention. And ironically, despite its name, less than 3 percent of the Centers for Disease Control and Prevention's 2008 budget is allocated toward chronic disease prevention, although its own "Third Report of the National Cholesterol Education Program's Adult Treatment Panel" (ATP III) recommends the use of therapeutic lifestyle changes and medical nutrition therapy to reduce the risk for chronic heart disease.

Fortunately, the balance has begun to shift. A recent MetLife [Insurance Company] survey found more than a quarter of all employers offer some type of wellness benefit. And Medicare beneficiaries are now entitled to a one-time physical examination, key screenings, and nutritional and smoking cessation counseling and other wellness benefits. However, these are very limited. For example, cardiovascular screening will be covered only once every five years. Nutritional counseling will be covered only for patients already diagnosed with type 2 diabetes or kidney disease, and is limited to just three hours the first year and just two hours in subsequent years.

Notwithstanding, wide-scale savings (billions of dollars and, more importantly, hundreds of thousands of lives) derived from therapeutic lifestyle changes (TLC) have been amply demonstrated.

For example:

- Implementing Stanford University's six-week Arthritis Self-Help Course among just 10,000 people with arthritis could save $2.6 million over four years, primarily through reduced physician visits.

- A sustained 10 percent weight loss will reduce an over-weight person's lifetime medical costs by $2,200–$5,300 through lower costs associated with hypertension, type 2 diabetes, heart disease, stroke and high cholesterol.

- A reduction of 12–13 mm Hg in systolic blood pressure is associated with a 21 percent reduction in coronary heart disease, a 37 percent reduction in stroke, a 25 percent reduction in total cardiovascular disease deaths and a 13 percent reduction in overall death rates.

Doctors Must Do More

A recent American Heart Association (AHA) survey of cardi-ologists and primary care physicians revealed the following:

- Only one in 10 respondents were successful in helping their patients achieve healthy serum lipid levels.

- Only half of respondents said they were very knowl-edgeable about the use of lifestyle interventions to lower serum lipids.

- Few considered being overweight or having a sedentary lifestyle as important contributors to coronary heart disease.

- Dietary and lifestyle interventions were viewed as only somewhat or moderately effective.

- Respondents cited lack of patient compliance and office visit time as major obstacles in implementing the ATP III guidelines.

In his 2005 presidential address to the AHA, endocrinolo-gist and researcher Dr. Robert Eckel challenged his colleagues to change these attitudes, saying, "We have an unprecedented arsenal of weapons [to prevent cardiovascular disease], includ-

Lifestyle Changes Can Improve Health

Obese and overweight individuals suffering metabolic syndrome and Type 2 diabetes showed significant health improvements after only three weeks of diet and moderate exercise even though the participants remained overweight.

"The study shows, contrary to common belief, that Type 2 diabetes and metabolic syndrome can be reversed solely through lifestyle changes," according to lead researcher Christian Roberts of University of California, Los Angeles. . . .

"The diet, combined with moderate exercise, improved many factors that contribute to heart disease and that are indirect measures of plaque progression in the arteries, including insulin resistance, high cholesterol, and markers of developing atherosclerosis," Roberts said. "The approach used in this experiment of combining exercise with a diet of unlimited calories is unusual."

"Study Finds Short-Term Lifestyle Changes
Improve Health Even Without Major Weight Loss,"
American Physiological Society, January 10, 2006,
www.the-aps.org.

ing many potent medications. However, this power is not enough and, in fact, in some cases, it has led us to ignore some very simple, effective and human measures." At the very heart of these measures are TLC.

Advice for Health Care Workers

Health care practitioners who appreciate the value of TLC and want to incorporate them into their practices must find ways to address the issues of communication, patient compliance, time management and financial reimbursement. These challenges could be overcome by taking several steps:

- *Take time to ask patients about their lifestyles.* A recent University of California San Francisco and Stanford University study concluded that most patients (especially those who are overweight or obese) want more support for weight management from their doctors, including dietary advice, help with setting realistic goals and exercise recommendations. Asking your patients about their lifestyles will not only open the door for a discussion of TLC; it also might instill in them a sense of urgency in following your recommendations.

- *Closely monitor results.* Regular follow-up visits are essential to the success of any TLC program. Follow-up visits allow progress to be monitored and adjustments to he made. Bioelectrical impedance analysis (BIA) offers a non-invasive option for measuring body composition, body mass index and other key indicators of health, with immediate results.

- *Assemble a TLC team.* Allied health professionals such as nurses, dieticians, fitness professionals or others experienced in health coaching or consulting can bring valuable skills and knowledge, including educating and inspiring patients regarding diet and lifestyle changes, conducting screenings and tracking progress.

- *Integrate TLC into the office flow.* Administrative staff members can schedule follow-up appointments, explain how the program works, advise patients regarding reimbursement issues (including insurance coverage, employer-sponsored reimbursement accounts or health savings accounts) and prepare educational handouts such as eating plans, exercise logs, etc.

A scientific statement from the Collaborative Writing Committee comprised of the American Cancer Society, the American Diabetes Association, and the AHA concluded that TLC represents a "new opportunity" for clinicians to target important risk factors and effect positive outcomes in the prevention and management of leading chronic conditions.

"*[In 2002, of the] estimated ninety thousand deaths annually in U.S. hospitals owing to bacterial infection, more than seventy per cent had been caused by organisms that were resistant to . . . drugs commonly used to treat them.*"

Antibiotic Resistant Bacteria Pose a Significant Threat to Health

Jerome Groopman

In the following viewpoint, Jerome Groopman reports on a class of bacteria known as gram-negative that is developing resistance to every known antibiotic. Although not as well known as methicillin-resistant Staphylococcus aureus *(MRSA), gram-negative bacteria such as* Klebsiella *are even more dangerous because there is no treatment for them, and they kill most people who are infected. Scientists are worried that the world will return to a "preantibiotic era" in the near future. Groopman, a medical doctor who has been the medical and science writer at* The New Yorker *since 1998, is the author of the 2007 book* How Doctors Think.

Jerome Groopman, "Superbugs," *The New Yorker*, August 11, 2008. © 2008 by Jerome Groopman. Originally published by The New Yorker, August 2008. Reprinted by permission of William Morris Agency, LLC, on behalf of the author.

As you read, consider the following questions:

1. What made the I.C.U. at Tisch Hospital an ideal environment for a highly infectious bacterium to spread?

2. Where were the first deaths from MRSA in community settings, according to the viewpoint?

3. According to Dr. Stuart Levy, what are the primary changes in bacteria that make them resistant to antibiotics?

In August, 2000, Dr. Roger Wetherbee, an infectious-disease expert at New York University's Tisch Hospital, received a disturbing call from the hospital's microbiology laboratory. At the time, Wetherbee was in charge of handling outbreaks of dangerous microbes in the hospital, and the laboratory had isolated a bacterium called *Klebsiella pneumoniae* from a patient in an intensive-care unit [I.C.U.]. "It was literally resistant to every meaningful antibiotic that we had," Wetherbee recalled. . . . The microbe was sensitive only to a drug called colistin, which had been developed decades earlier and largely abandoned as a systemic treatment, because it can severely damage the kidneys. "So we had this report, and I looked at it and said to myself, 'My God, this is an organism that basically we can't treat.'"

A Dangerous Bacterium

Klebsiella is in a class of bacteria called gram-negative, based on its failure to pick up the dye in a Gram's stain test. (Gram-positive organisms, which include *Streptococcus* and *Staphylococcus*, have a different cellular structure.) It inhabits both humans and animals and can survive in water and on inanimate objects. We can carry it on our skin and in our noses and throats, but it is most often found in our stool, and fecal contamination on the hands of caregivers is the most frequent source of infection among patients. Healthy people can harbor *Klebsiella* to no detrimental effect; those with debilitating conditions, like liver disease or severe diabetes, or those recovering from major surgery, are most likely to fall ill. The bacterium is oval in shape, resembling a TicTac, and has a thick, sugar-filled outer coat, which makes it difficult for white blood cells to engulf and destroy it. Fimbria—fine, hairlike extensions that enable *Klebsiella* to adhere to the lining of the throat, trachea, and bronchi—project from the bacteria's surface; the attached microbes can travel deep into our lungs, where they destroy the delicate alveoli, the air sacs that allow us to obtain oxygen. The resulting hemorrhage produces a blood-filled sputum, nicknamed "currant jelly." *Klebsiella* can also attach to the urinary tract and infect the kidneys. When the bacteria enter the bloodstream, they release a fatty substance known as an endotoxin, which injures the lining of the blood vessels and can cause fatal shock.

Tisch Hospital has four intensive-care units, all in the east wing on the fifteenth floor, and at the time of the outbreak there were thirty-two intensive-care beds. The I.C.U.s [Intensive Care Units] were built in 1961, and although the equipment had been modernized over the years, the units had otherwise remained relatively unchanged: the beds were close to each other, with I.V. [intravenous] pumps and respirators between them, and doctors and nursing staff were shared among the various I.C.U.s. This was an ideal environment for a highly infectious bacterium.

It was the first major outbreak of this multidrug-resistant strain of *Klebsiella* in the United States, and Wetherbee was concerned that the bacterium had become so well adapted in the I.C.U. that it could not be killed with the usual ammonia and phenol disinfectants. Only bleach seemed able to destroy it. Wetherbee and his team instructed doctors, nurses, and custodial staff to perform meticulous hand washing, and had them wear gowns and gloves when attending to infected patients. He instituted strict protocols to ensure that gloves were changed and hands vigorously disinfected after handling the tubing on each patient's ventilator. Spray bottles with bleach solutions were installed in the I.C.U.s, and surfaces and equipment were cleaned several times a day. Nevertheless, in the ensuing months *Klebsiella* infected more than a dozen patients.

Stringent Decontamination

In late autumn of 2000, in addition to pneumonia, patients began contracting urinary-tract and bloodstream infections from *Klebsiella*. The latter are often lethal, since once *Klebsiella* infects the bloodstream it can spread to every organ in the body. Wetherbee reviewed procedures in the I.C.U. again and discovered that the Foley catheters, used to drain urine from the bladder, had become a common source of contamination; when emptying the urine bags, staff members inadvertently splashed infected urine onto their gloves and onto nearby machinery. "They were very effectively moving the organism from one bed to the next," Wetherbee said. He ordered all the I.C.U.s to be decontaminated; the patients were temporarily moved out, supplies discarded, curtains changed, and each room was cleaned from floor to ceiling with a bleach solution. Even so, of the thirty-four patients with infections that year, nearly half died. The outbreak subsided in October, 2003, after even more stringent procedures for decontamination and hygiene were instituted: patients kept in isolation, and staff and visitors required to wear gloves, masks, and gowns at all times.

"My basic premise," Wetherbee said, "is that you take a capable microörganism like *Klebsiella* and you put it through the gruelling test of being exposed to a broad spectrum of antibiotics and it will eventually defeat your efforts, as this one did." Although Tisch Hospital has not had another outbreak, the bacteria appeared soon after at several hospitals in Brooklyn and one in Queens. When I spoke to infectious-disease experts this spring [2008], I was told that the resistant *Klebsiella* had also appeared at Mt. Sinai Medical Center, in Manhattan, and in hospitals in New Jersey, Pennsylvania, Cleveland, and St. Louis.

The Spread of MRSA

Of the so-called superbugs—those bacteria that have developed immunity to a wide number of antibiotics—the methicillin-resistant *Staphylococcus aureus*, or MRSA, is the most well known. Dr. Robert Moellering, a professor at Harvard Medical School, a past president of the Infectious Diseases Society of America, and a leading expert on antibiotic resistance, pointed out that MRSA, like *Klebsiella*, originally occurred in I.C.U.s, especially among patients who had undergone major surgery. "Until about ten years ago," Moellering told me, "virtually all cases of MRSA were either in hospitals or nursing homes. In the hospital setting, they cause wound infections after surgery, pneumonias, and bloodstream infections from indwelling catheters. But they can cause a variety of other infections, all the way to bacterial meningitis." The first deaths from MRSA in community settings, reported at the end of the nineteen-nineties, were among children in North Dakota and Minnesota. "And then it started showing up in men who have sex with men," Moellering said. "Soon, it began to be spread in prisons among the prisoners. Now we see it in a whole bunch of other populations." An outbreak among the St. Louis Rams football team, passed on through shared equipment, particularly affected the team's linemen; artificial turf, which causes skin abrasions that are prone to infection, exacerbated the problem. Other outbreaks were reported among insular religious groups in rural New York; Hurricane Katrina evacuees; and illegal tattoo recipients. "And now it's basically everybody," Moellering said. The deadly toxin produced by the strain of MRSA found in U.S. communities, Panton-Valentine leukocidin, is thought to destroy the membranes of white blood cells, damaging the body's primary defense against the microbe. In 2006, the Centers for Disease Control and Prevention [C.D.C.] recorded some nineteen thousand deaths and a hundred and five thousand infections from MRSA.

Unlike resistant forms of *Klebsiella* and other gram-negative bacteria, however, MRSA can be treated. "There are about a dozen new antibiotics coming on the market in the next couple of years," Moellering noted. "But there are no good drugs coming along for these gram-negatives." *Klebsiella* and similarly classified bacteria, including *Acinetobacter*, *Enterobacter*, and *Pseudomonas*, have an extra cellular envelope that MRSA lacks, and that hampers the entry of large molecules like antibiotic drugs. "The *Klebsiella* that caused particular trouble in New York are spreading out," Moellering told me. "They have very high mortality rates. They are sort of the doomsday-scenario bugs." . . .

Ten years ago [1998], the Institute of Medicine of the National Academy of Sciences, in Washington, D.C., assessed the economic impact of resistant microbes in the United States at up to five billion dollars, and experts now believe the figure to be much higher. In July, 2004, the Infectious Diseases Society of America released a white paper, "Bad Bugs, No Drugs: As Antibiotic Discovery Stagnates . . . A Public Health Crisis Brews," citing 2002 C.D.C. data showing that, of that year's estimated ninety thousand deaths annually in U.S. hospitals owing to bacterial infection, more than seventy per cent had been caused by organisms that were resistant to at least one of the drugs commonly used to treat them. Drawing on these data, collected mostly from hospitals in large urban areas which are affiliated with medical schools, the Centers for Disease Control and Prevention found more than a hundred thousand cases of gram-negative antibiotic-resistant bacteria. No precise numbers for all infections, including those outside hospitals, have been calculated, but the C.D.C. also reported that, among gram-negative hospital-acquired infections, about twenty per cent were resistant to state-of-the-art drugs.

How Bacteria Become Drug Resistant

In April [2008], I visited Dr. Stuart Levy, at Tufts University School of Medicine. Levy is a researcher-physician who has made key discoveries about how bacteria become resistant to antibiotics. In addition to the natural cell envelope of *Klebsiella*, Levy outlined three primary changes in bacteria that make them resistant to antibiotics. Each change involves either a mutation in the bacterium's own DNA or the importation of mutated DNA from another. (Bacteria can exchange DNA in the form of plasmids, molecules that are shared by the microbes and allow them to survive inhibitory antibiotics.) First, the bacteria may acquire an enzyme that can either act like a pair of scissors, cutting the drug into an inactive form, or modify the drug's chemical structure, so that it is rendered impotent. Thirty years ago, Levy discovered a second change: pumps inside the bacteria that could spit out the antibiotic once it had passed through the cell wall. His first reports were met with profound skepticism, but now, Levy told me, "most people would say that efflux is the most common form of bacterial resistance to antibiotics." The third change involves mutations that alter the inner contents of the microbe, so that the antibiotic can no longer inactivate its target.

Global studies have shown how quickly these bacteria can develop and spread. "This has been a problem in Mediterranean Europe that started about ten years ago," Dr. Christian Giske told me. Giske is a clinical microbiologist at Karolinska University Hospital, in Stockholm, who, with researchers in Israel and Denmark, recently reported on the worldwide spread of resistant gram-negative bacteria. He continued, "It started to get really serious during the last five or six years and has become really dramatic in Greece." A decade ago, only a few microbes in Southern Europe had multidrug resistance; now some fifty to sixty per cent of hospital-acquired infections are resistant.

Giske and his colleagues found that infection with a resistant strain of *Pseudomonas* increased, twofold to fivefold, a patient's risk of dying, and increased about twofold the patient's hospital stay. Like other exports in the field, Giske's team was concerned about the lack of new antibiotics being developed to combat gram-negative bacteria. "There are now a growing number of reports of cases of infections caused by gram-negative organisms for which no adequate therapeutic options exist," Giske and his colleagues wrote. "This return to the preantibiotic era has become a reality in many parts of the world."

Doctors and researchers fear that these bacteria may become entrenched in hospitals, threatening any patient who has significant health issues. "Anytime you hear about some kid getting snatched, you want to find something in that story that will convince you that that family is different from yours," Dr. Louis Rice, an expert in antibiotic resistance at Louis Stokes Cleveland VA Medical Center, told me. "But the problem is that any of us could be an I.C.U. patient tomorrow. It's not easy to convey this to people if it's not immediately a threat. You don't want to think about it. But it's actually anybody who goes into a hospital. This is scary stuff."

| "Experts say good, old-fashioned personal hygiene is the best defense against the increase of antibiotic-resistant staph infections—along with plenty of other bugs."

Antibiotic Resistant Infections Can Be Prevented

Ridgely Ochs

In the following viewpoint, Ridgely Ochs reports on cases of methicillin-resistant Staphylococcus aureus *infections on Long Island. An expert at the Centers for Disease Control and Prevention asserts that simple hygiene such as hand washing will prevent the spread of MRSA, a disease that is more deadly when acquired in the hospital than in the community. Ochs summarizes that if hospitals are highly aggressive in their approach to hygiene, they can prevent most MRSA infections. Ochs is a deputy editor of* Newsday.

As you read, consider the following questions:

1. What percentage of men say they wash their hands after using a public restroom?
2. On average, how often should health care workers in intensive care units wash their hands?

3. What nineteenth-century nurse led the effort to make hospitals cleaner?

L isten to your mother: Wash your hands.

Experts say good, old-fashioned personal hygiene is the best defense against the increase of antibiotic-resistant staph infections—along with plenty of other bugs.

Dr. John Jernigan, an expert at the Centers for Disease Control and Prevention [CDC] on MRSA—or methicillin-resistant *Staphylococcus aureus*—said that clusters of antibiotic-resistant staph infections in the community "go away when those involved implement simple hygiene measures."

On Long Island, several school districts have reported cases of MRSA, and a 12-year-old Brooklyn boy died two weeks ago after getting an MRSA infection.

Despite the mounting concerns in the community, Jernigan says it is nevertheless unnecessary for school districts to shut down to disinfect. Instead, he said, they need to make sure students clean their hands, cover any sores or wounds with a clean dressing, and don't share personal products like towels or razors.

The reason: Staph infections, including MRSA, are "primarily spread by skin-to-skin contact and the role of the contaminated environment is not that important," Jernigan said.

The Role of Hand Washing

It wasn't until the 19th century that doctors began to understand the role of hand-washing in preventing the spread of disease. In the 1840s, a Viennese doctor observed that women whose babies were delivered by doctors were dying in childbirth at a higher rate than those delivered by midwives. Many of the doctors were coming to the obstetrics ward directly from the autopsy room.

When he insisted doctors clean their hands before treating patients, the death rate plunged.

Although the good-hygiene message is old and irrefutable, plenty of evidence suggests that people ignore it. A 2005 study found that while 91 percent of Americans say they always wash their hands after using a public rest room, only 83 percent did. Men were worse than women: 90 percent of women washed their hands while 75 percent of men did.

Perhaps more troubling, studies cited by the CDC show that on average 40 percent of health care workers comply with good hand hygiene practices. And doctors are worse than nurses, the studies have found.

The CDC studies agree that MRSA is more prevalent and potentially more serious when acquired in the hospital than when contracted outside, in the community. That is because people in the hospital are sicker. And they may undergo invasive procedures—they may have a central line catheter inserted or go on a ventilator—which can become portals for MRSA to enter the body and cause a potentially deadly infection.

But it's not easy to get health care workers to clean their hands again and again when they come in contact so frequently with patients. One study found that the lowest adherence rate to hand-washing occurred in intensive care units. There, health care workers needed on average to wash hands up to 20 times per hour.

"It is almost always the case that the errant health care worker is either completely absorbed in the task at hand, or simply is unaware of the potential impact of the consequence of noncompliance," said Dr. Susan Donelan, medical director of the health care epidemiology department at Stony Brook University Medical Center.

Aggressive Hygiene Can Greatly Reduce Infections

But experts said that if hospitals are aggressive they can greatly reduce infection rates.

Hand Washing Prevents Infection

Hand washing is a vital first-line defense against hospital-acquired infections, and studies done decades ago established a direct correlation between hand washing and significant reductions in infection rates. The CDC [Centers for Disease Control] reports that thorough hand washing could save as many as 20,000 lives a year. A careful washing of the hands consumes only seconds of a healthcare worker's time and costs literally pennies to the institution. And the costs of *not* doing it are huge: the expense of hospital-acquired infections is now reaching into the billions of dollars; the loss of human life is incalculable. Consequently, a practice of stringently enforcing hand-washing rules would appear to be a no-brainer.

Dr. Julia A. Hallisy,
The Empowered Patient: Hundreds of Life-Saving
Facts, Action Steps and Strategies You Need to Know.
Bold Spirit Press, 2007, p. 46.

Dr. Don Goldmann, senior vice president of the Institute for Healthcare Improvement, a not-for-profit group, said that if hospitals follow good hygiene practices 95 percent of the time and are rigorous in the correct use of ventilators and catheters, "I think we would look around in amazement and say, 'What happened to that problem?'"

Joseph Conte, head of quality management at North Shore-Long Island Jewish Health System, said patients should ask their doctors about a hospital's infection rate for a particular procedure. "If they cannot give the answer, it's not good," he said. "You want to be in a place where people are cognizant. It's everybody's job."

Getting people to focus on the issue is the first step, Conte said. About eight months ago [around February 2007] they began placing bottles of alcohol hand sanitizers and signs in 17 languages reminding people to clean their hands all over the system's 15 hospitals. The system's 40,000 computers have a screen saver with the same message, Conte said.

The reminders seem to be working. When the bottles were first put out, they would last for a month, Conte said. "Now," he said, "they're gone within a couple of days." . . .

A History of Hygiene

- *In antiquity*. Public baths popular in ancient Greece and Rome. Traditions such as Turkish baths, which combined religious purification and hygiene, eventually developed. Chamber pot first appeared in ancient Rome.

- *In the Middle Ages*. Public baths were still popular, but this is known as a fetid era of streets with running sewage and roaming animals.

- *The Renaissance*. Ignorance about disease led to the belief that a layer of grime on the body protected people from the plague. People believed that water made them ill by penetrating the pores of their skin.

- *The 18th century*. First toothpaste developed.

- *The 19th century*. With the discovery of the germ theory, progress dawns. Many new buildings had septic tanks. The availability of cheap cotton clothing allows clothes to be easily washed—as opposed to woolens. Conferences on hygiene are held. Quarantines are introduced. Deaths associated with surgery plummeted as doctors washed their hands. Nurse Florence Nightingale leads effort to make hospitals cleaner.

- *20th century.* New antibiotics—and better cleanliness standards—lead to drops in maternal and infant mortality, and longevity steadily rises. Traditional measures became conventional wisdom: reasonable exposure to the sun and fresh air, and isolation of sick people during epidemics. Portable water, public rest rooms more widely available.

- *21st century.* Some antibiotic-resistant bacteria become more widespread. An industry develops around what are known as "hygienic surfaces" that kill bacteria.

Periodical Bibliography

The following articles have been selected to supplement the diverse views presented in this chapter.

Sandy Bauers "Concerns Mount Over Ingredient in Plastics; Chemical Industry Disputes Claim that BPA Poses Health Risks," *The Buffalo News*, May 11, 2008.

Jay Cao "Nutrition from the Labs: Connecting the Dots: Obesity to Osteoporosis," *Grand Forks Herald*, October 1, 2008.

John Carey "Heart Disease: Not About Cholesterol?" *Business Week Online*, April 16, 2008.

Centers for Disease Control and Prevention "Heart Disease," September 2008, www.cdc.gov.

Dan Childs "Largest Ever Recorded Decline in Cancer Deaths," *ABC News*, January 17, 2007, http://abcnews.go.com.

Daniel J. DeNoon "Bird Flu Jumped from Son to Father," *WebMD Health News*, April 7, 2008, www.medicinenet.com.

Andrea Gawrylewski "MRSA: RIP?" *The Scientist*, December 11, 2007, www.thescientist.com.

Jay Herson "The Coming Osteoporosis Epidemic," *The Futurist*, Vol. 41, No. 2, March-April 2007.

CHAPTER 2

What Human Behaviors Contribute to or Damage Health?

Chapter Preface

Medical researchers have long suggested that some serious health problems are the result of behaviors that either cause disease or exacerbate underlying health problems. For example, most scientists agree that smoking cigarettes leads to lung damage in the form of cancer, emphysema, and other respiratory illnesses. Likewise, researchers also claim that cardiovascular disease could be avoided or improved if people would watch their diets and exercise moderately.

Another behavior that some researchers suggest may cause long-term health risks is the usage of cellular phones. Vini Gautam Khurana, a neurosurgeon, argues in the 2008 article "Mobile Phones and Brain Tumours," that cell phones emit dangerous electromagnetic radiation that, over time, will cause brain tumors. He writes, "There is a growing and statistically significant body of evidence reporting that brain tumours . . . are associated with 'heavy' and 'prolonged' mobile phone use, particularly on the same side as the 'preferred ear' for telephony." In addition, he asserts that Bluetooth devices and unshielded headsets also harm the user by using the head as an antenna.

On the other hand, the American Cancer Society reports in a May 28, 2008, article, "Cellular Phones," that although cell phones are a new technology that have not yet been extensively studied, there is little indication that they cause brain tumors. They cite several case-controlled studies in which the cell phone use of patients with brain cancer was compared with the cell phone use of a control group. The studies do not demonstrate a higher incidence of brain cancer among cell phone users. Likewise, the studies do not show that an increased use of cell phones increases the risk of brain cancer.

Finally, the studies do not show a correlation between the side of the head the brain cancer occurred on and the preferred ear for telephony.

Regardless of whether cell phone use causes brain cancer, there is incontrovertible evidence that cell phone usage endangers human health by substantially increasing the risk of car accidents by those who talk on cell phones while driving. A 2009 Fact Sheet from the National Safety Council reports that cell phone usage "contributes to 636,000 crashes, 330,000 injuries, 12,000 serious injuries, and 2,600 deaths each year." Similarly, *Science Daily* reported on January 27, 2009, that a University of Alabama study demonstrates that "children who talk on cell phones while crossing streets are at a higher risk for injuries or death in a pedestrian accident."

As studies about cell phone usage and human health increase, a growing body of evidence will clarify both the positive and negative nature of this technology. Like many other human behaviors, using a cell phone can be a beneficial or detrimental action, depending on circumstances. Likewise, the writers of the following viewpoints address tobacco use, tanning beds, exercise, and obesity, arguing from differing perspectives.

| "Being overweight is actually a medical concern because it can seriously affect a person's health."

Obesity Poses a Serious Health Risk

TeensHealth.org

In the following viewpoint, Mary L. Gavin and the editors of TeensHealth argue that being overweight is not only a matter of appearance but also a matter for health. Gavin reports that young people are experiencing health problems that used to be limited to adults. She also asserts that genetics, food choices, and emotional eating contribute to obesity. She lists many health issues associated with obesity before concluding that it is never too late for change. Gavin is a pediatrician and the medical editor of KidsHealth *and* TeensHealth *Web sites.*

As you read, consider the following questions:

1. What examples does Gavin offer of health problems that used to affect only adults and now are affecting younger people?

2. What is the name of the condition where people temporarily stop breathing during sleep?

3. What are the technical term and symptoms for a rare cause of severe headaches in obese teens and adults, according to the viewpoint?

In our looks-obsessed society, lots of people think that being overweight is an appearance issue. But being overweight is actually a medical concern because it can seriously affect a person's health.

The health problems that stem from being overweight go way beyond the ones we usually hear about, like diabetes and heart disease. Being overweight can also affect a person's joints, breathing, sleep, mood, and energy levels. So being overweight can impact a person's entire quality of life.

Defining Overweight

When people eat more calories than they burn off, their bodies store the extra calories as fat.

A couple of pounds of extra body fat are not a health risk for most people. But when people keep up a pattern of eating more calories than they burn, more and more fat builds up in their bodies.

Eventually, the body gets to a point where the amount of body fat can have a negative effect on a person's health. Doctors use the terms "overweight" or "obese" to describe when someone is at greatest risk of developing weight-related health problems.

As you've probably heard, more people are overweight today than ever before. Experts are calling this an "obesity epidemic." This health problem affects young people as well as adults—one third of all kids between the ages of 2 and 19 are overweight or obese. So younger people are now developing health problems that used to affect only adults, like high blood pressure, high cholesterol, and type 2 diabetes.

Why Do People Become Overweight?

Obesity tends to run in families. Some people have a genetic tendency to gain weight more easily than others because they burn calories more slowly. During times when food was scarce, this was a real advantage. But now that food is available 24/7 in most industrialized countries, an efficient metabolism that once ensured our survival now works to our disadvantage.

Although genes strongly influence body type and size, the environment also plays a role. People today may be gaining weight because of unhealthy food choices (like fast food) and family habits (like eating in front of the television instead of around a table). High-calorie, low-nutrient snacks and beverages, bigger portions of food, and less-active lifestyles are all contributing to the obesity epidemic.

Sometimes people turn to food for emotional reasons, such as when they feel upset, anxious, sad, stressed out, or even bored. When this happens, they often eat more than they need.

Figuring out if a teen is overweight can be more complicated than it is for adults. That's because teens are still growing and developing.

Doctors and other health care professionals often use a measurement called body mass index (BMI) to determine if someone is overweight.

Doctors consider a teen *obese* when his or her BMI number is higher than the BMI numbers of 95% of other teens the same age and gender. Someone whose BMI number is between 85% and 95% of the BMIs of other teens the same age and gender is *overweight*.

Health Problems of Being Overweight

Obesity is bad news for both body and mind. Not only can it make a person feel tired and uncomfortable, carrying extra

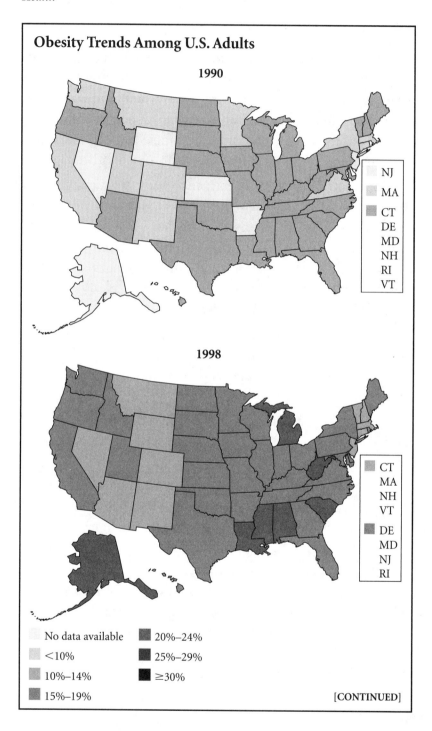

Obesity Trends Among U.S. Adults

1990

NJ
MA
CT
DE
MD
NH
RI
VT

1998

CT
MA
NH
VT

DE
MD
NJ
RI

No data available   20%–24%

<10%   25%–29%

10%–14%   ≥30%

15%–19%

[CONTINUED]

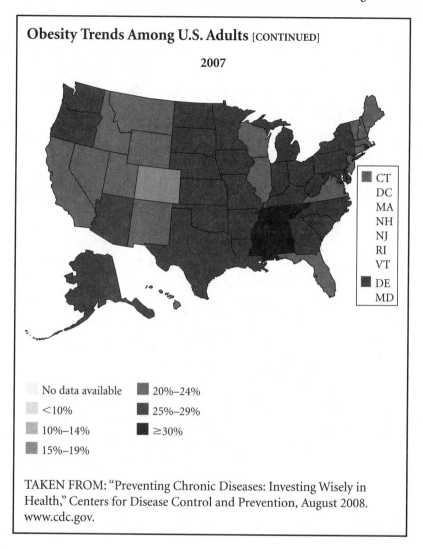

Obesity Trends Among U.S. Adults [CONTINUED]

2007

CT
DC
MA
NH
NJ
RI
VT
DE
MD

No data available   20%–24%

<10%   25%–29%

10%–14%   ≥30%

15%–19%

TAKEN FROM: "Preventing Chronic Diseases: Investing Wisely in Health," Centers for Disease Control and Prevention, August 2008. www.cdc.gov.

weight puts added stress on the body, especially the bones and joints of the legs. As they get older, kids and teens who are overweight are more likely to develop diabetes and heart disease.

The health problems that affect overweight teens include:

- *Blount's disease.* Excess weight on growing bones can lead to this bone deformity of the lower legs.

- *Arthritis.* Wear and tear on the joints from carrying extra weight can cause this painful joint problem at a young age.

- *Slipped capital femoral epiphyses (SCFE).* Obese children and teens are at greater risk for this painful hip problem. SCFE requires immediate attention and surgery to prevent further damage to the joint.

- *Asthma.* Obesity is associated with breathing problems that can make it harder to keep up with friends, play sports, or just walk from class to class.

- *Sleep apnea.* This condition (where a person temporarily stops breathing during sleep) is a serious problem for many overweight kids and adults. Not only does it interrupt sleep, sleep apnea can leave people feeling tired and affect their ability to concentrate and learn. It also may lead to heart problems.

- *High blood pressure.* When blood pressure is high, the heart must pump harder and the arteries must carry blood that's moving under greater pressure. If the problem continues for a long time, the heart and arteries may no longer work as well as they should. Although rare in most teens, high blood pressure, or hypertension, is more common in overweight or obese teens.

- *High cholesterol.* Long before getting sick, obese teens may have abnormal blood lipid levels, including high cholesterol, low HDL ("good") cholesterol, and high triglyceride levels. These increase the risk of heart attack and stroke when a person gets older.

- *Gallstones.* An accumulation of bile that hardens in the gallbladder forms gallstones. These may be painful and require surgery.

- *Fatty liver.* When fat accumulates in the liver, it can cause inflammation, scarring, and permanent liver damage.

- *Pseudotumor cerebri.* This is a rare cause of severe headaches in obese teens and adults. There is no tumor, but pressure builds in the brain. In addition to headaches, symptoms may include vomiting, an unsteady way of walking, and vision problems that may become permanent if not treated.

- *Polycystic ovary syndrome (PCOS).* Girls who are overweight may miss periods—or not get their periods at all—and may have elevated testosterone (the male hormone) levels in the blood. Although it is normal for girls to have some testosterone in their blood, too much can interfere with normal ovulation and may cause excess hair growth, worsening acne, and male-type baldness. PCOS is associated with insulin resistance, a precursor to developing type 2 diabetes. Women who are overweight also might have fertility problems.

- *Insulin resistance and diabetes.* When there is excess body fat, insulin is less effective at getting glucose, the body's main source of energy, into cells. More insulin becomes needed to maintain a normal blood sugar. For some overweight teens, insulin resistance may progress to diabetes (high blood sugar).

- *Depression.* People who are obese are more likely to be depressed and have lower self-esteem.

Luckily, it's never too late to make changes that can effectively control weight and the health problems it causes. Those changes don't have to be big. For a start, make a plan to cut back on sugary beverages, pass up on seconds, and get more exercise, even if it's just 5–10 minutes a day. Build your way up to big changes by making a series of small ones. And don't be afraid to ask for help!

"The claims about the [United King-
dom] and [United States] obesity
'epidemics' are wildly exaggerated
and—more seriously—deliberately
skewed."

The Health Risks of Obesity Have Been Exaggerated

Patrick Basham and Jane Feinman

*In the following viewpoint, Patrick Basham argues in an inter-
view with Jane Feinman that there is no obesity epidemic.
Rather, he asserts that politicians and the diet industry have
manipulated statistics to make it appear as if the number of
people who are obese has increased dramatically. He further argues that there is no evidence of a childhood obesity epidemic,
and he asserts that current programs to curb obesity do children
more harm than good. Basham is a professor at Johns Hopkins
University and the author of* Diet Nation *(2006). Feinman is a
British journalist.*

As you read, consider the following questions:

1. What happened in 1997 to the BMI classification of being overweight, according to Basham?

2. In 2004, a study by the Centers for Disease Control and Prevention (CDC) claimed that nearly 400,000 deaths were attributable to diet; the following year, the CDC and the National Institutes of Health put the number of annual deaths from overweight and obesity at what figure?

3. What problems have adult attempts to control children's eating patterns created, according to Basham?

Being fat has suddenly become politically unacceptable. According to the [United Kingdom's] Health Secretary, Alan Johnson, obesity is a "potential crisis on the scale of climate change", while the US Surgeon General has described it as "a greater threat than weapons of mass destruction".

Professor Philip James, chair of the International Obesity Task Force, raised the alarm in the UK two years ago [2005], when he warned that an "unprecedented epidemic of life-threatening obesity" had taken off in the Eighties. And [in October 2007] the Prime Minister [Gordon Brown] earmarked funding for "a long-term action plan to fight obesity"—after the Government-commissioned Foresight report found that half the population will be clinically obese within 25 years, and that, by 2050, obesity will cost the country £45bn a year.

The Obesity Scare

Such a response might make sense if there really was an epidemic rise in obesity. In fact, the claims about the UK and US obesity "epidemics" are wildly exaggerated and—more seriously—deliberately skewed.

Politicians have been taken in by a cottage industry that has developed around the obesity crusade; an industry that consists of a wide range of groups, from public-health bureaucrats to big business, including the pharmaceutical industry.

These organisations and individuals, with their need for ever-greater empires and funding, know only too well that warning of impending disaster captures the Government's attention. Yet in this classic case of spin, there are real victims: those people condemned by wrong-headed policies to a lifetime of yo-yo dieting and an unhealthy obsession with food and weight.

An analysis of the science behind the headlines reveals a very different picture. For a start, the claim that half of the British population will be clinically obese in 25 years assumes, without any empirical foundation, that every overweight child will become an overweight adult and that every overweight adult will progress to obesity.

It is true that Body Mass Index [BMI] (a figure consisting of height squared divided by weight squared) statistics show a significant increase in overweight adults over the past decade. But this is an extraordinary case of moving the methodological goalposts: in 1997, the BMI classification of being overweight was changed from 27 to 25. At a stroke, millions of people previously classed as normal suddenly became overweight, with no good reason to explain the change. This obscures the fact that the average adult weighs only a pound or two more than those of a generation ago. The increase in obesity applies only to the morbidly obese (with a BMI greater than 40), who make up less than 5 per cent of the obese.

There Is No Evidence for an Increase in Childhood Obesity

Further, there is not a shred of evidence to suggest that childhood obesity is on the increase, let alone accelerating. The Department of Health's own survey, published in December 2004, shows that for all children aged two to 15 there was actually a slight decline in obesity prevalence from 2004–2005. And in children aged 11–15, there was a 17.5 per cent decline. So, it is difficult to see from the Government's own data just where this talk of an obesity "epidemic" is coming from.

The "Obesity Epidemic" Is a Scam

When the [U.S.] government decided that obesity was "a critical health problem in this country that causes millions of Americans to suffer unnecessary health problems and to die prematurely," your right to decide what, where, and how much to eat disappeared.

The "obesity epidemic" is a scam. The players involved in it include animal rights advocates who want to disparage consumption of beef, chicken, pork, milk, cheese, and other nutritious foods that come from animals. Others include pharmaceutical companies who are either selling or developing drugs to deal with obesity or just weight loss.

Alan Caruba, "The Great Obesity Scam,"
Lincoln Heritage Institute, 2004, www.serve.com.

What's more, the latest UK *National Diet and Nutrition Survey* (2000) found that caloric intake in both boys and girls aged four to 18 declined since the previous survey in 1983. There is similar data in the [United] States: a study published in the *Journal of the American Medical Association* in 2004 found no statistically significant increase in the prevalence of overweight or obese children between 1999 and 2002.

Behind the medical profession's goal of identifying overweight people is the claim that it is unhealthy to be above normal weight. I am no obesity apologist: morbidly obese people are so fat that they are putting their lives at risk. But the claim that being overweight or modestly obese is associated with an increased risk of premature death has been discredited by a series of studies. For example, the 2004 US Centers for Disease Control and Prevention (CDC) study claimed that there were nearly 400,000 annual deaths attributable to diet and physical inactivity. Yet this was discredited the following year by a study from researchers at the CDC and the National Institutes of Health, which put the figure of annual deaths from overweight and obesity at just 25,814.

Even the alleged link between excessive food intake and childhood obesity has no scientific basis. A 2002 cross-cultural review of obesity in the US, France, Australia, Britain and Spain found little evidence that overweight or obese children and adolescents consumed more calories than others. At least one study has found that overweight children consume fewer calories than their thinner peers do.

Indeed, the whole idea of "good" food and "bad" food is increasingly open to question. It has long been known that consuming a high-fat diet does not necessarily raise blood cholesterol or reduce longevity—as can be seen by the fat-loving Dutch and East Africa's Masai. A recent series of studies has also shown that a low-fat diet has little effect on reducing the risk of breast cancer, colorectal cancer or cardiovascular disease in postmenopausal women.

There is also strong evidence that blaming childhood obesity on advertising is fatally flawed—and that banning advertising of junk food will have little or no effect on our children's weight. And research into the connection between food advertising and the size of the food market, both in Europe and the US, has found that advertising influences brand selection, but not diet.

The Obesity Crusade Is Dangerous

I am an independent academic and not a junk-food industry lobbyist. I am a passionate combatant in this debate, because I believe that the obesity crusade is dangerous. Virtually all the literature on dieting has concluded that attempts at weight loss are largely unsuccessful and, more worryingly, that there are health risks in such behaviour.

There are similar doubts over the efficacy of policies to counter childhood obesity, whether through changing school food, removing vending machines with "bad" food or increasing physical education.

In the States, an obesity prevention programme in 50 schools known as Catch (Child Adolescent Trial for Cardiovascular Health) found no statistically significant changes in the children's blood pressure, BMI or cholesterol levels. Such results are hardly surprising: several recent studies have shown that adult attempts to control children's eating patterns lead to children eating more—as well as raising the risk of body-image problems and eating disorders. It's this unintended, and uninvestigated, outcome of a weight-obsessed society that should be the cause for concern.

If we take into account the relatively few lives lost prematurely due to obesity, and compare them to the very significant health costs associated with both dieting and eating disorders, there is surely a compelling case that the damage to health from attempting to lose weight is far greater than the health consequences of overweight and obesity. Indeed, perhaps rather than a campaign against obesity, it is a war on thinness that is required.

| "It is hard to imagine a single practice with more health benefits than regular physical activity."

Exercise Can Benefit Health

National Heart, Lung, and Blood Institute

In the following viewpoint, the authors argue that physical activity and exercise have many potent health benefits. Conversely, they argue, inactivity increases the risk of chronic and serious diseases. Engaging in regular physical activity and exercise provides protection against heart disease by burning extra calories and lowering weight; reducing cholesterol; and lowering blood pressure, according to the authors. The National Heart, Lung, and Blood Institute is a member of the National Institutes of Health, the primary medical and behavioral research institution in the United States.

As you read, consider the following questions:

1. According to the authors, how much physical activity or exercise does an adult need to reduce the risk of heart disease?
2. How does a heart attack happen?
3. According to the authors, in addition to protecting the heart, staying active provides what other health benefits?

National Heart, Lung, and Blood Institute, "Physical Activity and Your Health," Your Guide to Physical Activity and Your Heart, June 2006. Reproduced by permission.

If you currently get regular physical activity, congratulations! But if you're not yet getting all the activity you need, you have lots of company. According to the Centers for Disease Control and Prevention (CDC), 60 percent of Americans are not meeting the recommended levels of physical activity. Fully 16 percent of Americans are not active at all. Overall, women tend to be less active than men, and older people are less likely to get regular physical activity than younger individuals.

What does it mean to get "regular physical activity"? To reduce the risk of heart disease, adults need only do about 30 minutes of moderate activity on most, and preferably all, days of the week. This level of activity can also lower your chances of having a stroke, colon cancer, high blood pressure, diabetes, and other medical problems.

If you're also trying to manage your weight and prevent gradual, unhealthy weight gain, try to get 60 minutes of moderate- to vigorous-intensity activity on most days of the week. At the same time, watch your calories. Take in only enough calories to maintain your weight. Those who are trying to keep weight off should aim a bit higher: Try to get 60–90 minutes of moderate-intensity activity daily, without taking in extra calories. . . .

If you're not as active as you might be, take a moment to consider why. Maybe you're just in the habit of traveling by car or bus, even when you're not going far. In your free time, perhaps it's tempting to sit down in front of the TV or computer rather than do something more vigorous. It's easy to get busy or tired and decide that it's just simpler to put off that brisk walk or bike ride. But when you think about the serious problems that physical inactivity can create for your health—and the enormous rewards of getting regular activity—you may want to reconsider. Let's start with the ways that physical activity affects your heart.

Inactivity Leads to Heart Disease

It's worth repeating: Physical inactivity greatly increases your risk of developing heart disease. Heart disease occurs when the arteries that supply blood to the heart muscle become hardened and narrowed, due to a buildup of plaque on the arteries' inner walls. Plaque is the accumulation of fat, cholesterol, and other substances. As plaque continues to build up in the arteries, blood flow to the heart is reduced.

Heart disease can lead to a heart attack. A heart attack happens when a cholesterol-rich plaque bursts and releases its contents into the bloodstream. This causes a blood clot to form over the plaque, totally blocking blood flow through the artery and preventing vital oxygen and nutrients from getting to the heart. A heart attack can cause permanent damage to the heart muscle.

Some people aren't too concerned about heart disease because they think it can be cured with surgery. This is a myth. Heart disease is a lifelong condition. It's true that certain procedures can help blood and oxygen flow more easily to the heart. But the arteries remain damaged, which means you are still more likely to have a heart attack. What's more, the condition of your blood vessels will steadily worsen unless you make changes in your daily habits and control other factors that increase risk.

Heart disease is a serious disease—and too often, a fatal one. It is the number one killer of Americans, with 500,000 people in the United States dying of heart disease each year. Many others with heart problems become permanently disabled. That's why it's so vital to take action to prevent this disease. Getting regular physical activity should be part of everyone's heart disease prevention program.

Heart Disease Risk Factors

Risk factors are conditions or habits that make a person more likely to develop a disease. They can also increase the chances

The Benefits of Activity

The health benefits of activity begin to kick in at around 100 calories a day. That's the equivalent of walking a mile or square-dancing for 15 to 30 minutes. The more energy you expend, the better.

A long-term study of Harvard University alumni showed the lowest death rates in those who burned about 300 calories a day in exercise or activity.

If you tend to be a sitter, adding "activity bits" . . . is a great way to start burning more calories, lower your risk of cardiovascular disease and keep you mobile.

Harvard Health Letters,
"No-Sweat Exercising: Keep Moving Through Your Day,"
The Record *(Bergen County, NJ), February 6, 2007.*

that an existing disease will get worse. Certain risk factors for heart disease, such as getting older or having a family history of early heart disease, can't be changed. But *physical inactivity is a major risk factor for heart disease that you have control over. . . .*

Other major risk factors for heart disease that you can change are smoking, high blood pressure, high blood cholesterol, overweight, and diabetes. . . . Every risk factor counts. Research shows that each individual risk factor greatly increases the chances of developing heart disease and having a heart attack. A damaged heart can damage your life, by interfering with enjoyable activities and even keeping you from doing simple things, such as taking a walk or climbing steps.

But it's important to know that you have a lot of power to protect your heart health. . . . Getting regular physical activity is an especially important part of your healthy heart program, because physical activity both directly reduces your heart disease risk *and* reduces your chances of developing other risk factors for heart disease. For example, regular physical activity may reduce LDL (bad) cholesterol, increase HDL (good) cholesterol, and lower high blood pressure. It can also protect your heart by helping to prevent and control diabetes. Finally, physical activity can help you to lose excess weight or stay at your desirable weight, which will also help to lower your risk of heart disease.

Physical Activity: The Calorie Connection

One way that regular physical activity protects against heart disease is by burning extra calories, which helps you to lose excess weight or stay at your desirable weight. To understand how physical activity affects calories, it is helpful to consider the concept of "energy balance." Energy balance is the amount of calories you take in relative to the amount of calories you burn. Per week, you need to burn off about 3,500 more calories than you take in to lose 1 pound. If you need to lose weight for your health, regular physical activity can help you through one of two approaches.

First, you can choose to eat your usual amount of calories, but be more active. For example, a 200-pound person who keeps on eating the same amount of calories, but begins to walk briskly each day for 1^1/$_2$ miles, will lose about 14 pounds in 1 year. Staying active will also help to keep the weight off.

Second, you can eat fewer calories and be more active. This is the best way to lose weight, since you're more likely to be successful by combining a healthful, lower-calorie diet with physical activity. For example, a 200-pound person who consumes 250 fewer calories per day, and begins to walk briskly each day for 1^1/$_2$ miles, will lose about 40 pounds in 1 year.

Most of the energy you burn each day—about three quarters of it—goes to activities that your body automatically engages in for survival, such as breathing, sleeping, and digesting food. The part of your energy output that *you* control is daily physical activity. Any activity you take part in beyond your body's automatic activities will burn extra calories. Even seated activities, such as using the computer or watching TV, will burn calories—but only a very small number. That's why it's important to make time each day for moderate-to-vigorous physical activity.

The Many Benefits of Exercise

It is hard to imagine a single practice with more health benefits than regular physical activity. In addition to protecting your heart in numerous ways, staying active:

- May help to prevent cancers of the breast, uterus, and colon.
- Strengthens your lungs and helps them to work more efficiently.
- Tones and strengthens your muscles.
- Builds stamina.
- Keeps your joints in good condition.
- Improves balance.
- May slow bone loss.

Regular physical activity can also boost the way you feel. It may:

- Give you more energy.
- Help you to relax and cope better with stress.
- Build confidence.

- Allow you to fall asleep more quickly and sleep more soundly.

- Help you to beat the blues.

- Provide an enjoyable way to share time with friends or family.

"EA [exercise addiction] can have serious, even fatal, long-term effects.

Exercise Can Be Harmfully Addictive

Edward J. Cumella

In the following viewpoint, the author argues that exercise addiction (EA) is a serious, often overlooked, health problem, particularly for young, female athletes and among some men suffering from a variety of body-image problems. According to the author, EA is sometimes linked to eating disorders and individuals who stand a greater risk of death. Therefore, health professionals must screen for EA and be prepared to offer treatment interventions to prevent injury and death. Edward J. Cumella, Ph.D., is director of research and education at Remuda Ranch Programs for Anorexia and Bulimia.

As you read, consider the following questions:

1. What are some of the medical complications of exercise addiction, according to the author?

2. What are the eight factors to consider in treating exercise addiction, according to the author?

Edward J. Cumella, "The Heavy Weight of Exercise Addiction," *Behavioral Health Management*, vol. 25, September-October 2005, pp. 26–28. Copyright © 2005 Medquest Communications, LLC. Republished with permission of Medquest Communications, LLC, conveyed through Copyright Clearance Center, Inc.

3. In what sports do athletes have the highest risk of exercise addiction relapse, according to the author?

Exercise addiction (EA) is a compulsion to exercise. By exercising, EA patients reduce anxiety about being or becoming overweight, body dissatisfaction, or appearance concerns. EA has addiction features because, like drugs, EA raises endorphin [brain chemical] levels. EA patients thus may experience feelings of well-being but with decreased awareness of emotional and physical pain and the serious, possibly permanent, health problems arising from their EA behavior. Although prevalence data are sparse, EA's greatest risk groups appear to include athletes in sports encouraging thinness or appearance standards, young and middle-age women, and young men.

EA is associated with eating disorders or stands alone. EA initially was recognized as a symptom of anorexia and bulimia, used to purge unwanted calories following binge, normal, or even minimal eating. Some eating disorder patients choose exercise as their purging method because they are incapable of inducing vomiting, find vomiting aversive, or see exercise as more socially acceptable. Clinicians describe eating disorder patients whose primary purging method is EA as having "anorexia athletica" or "exercise bulimia."

Excessive Exercise and Body Image

For female athletes, especially those in sports such as long-distance running in which low body weight may be beneficial, an eating disorder syndrome exists called the female- or elite-athlete triad. It consists of disordered eating, amenorrhea, [a cessation of the menstrual cycle], and osteoporosis [bone loss] in conjunction with exercise. Depending on symptoms and severity, it is diagnosed as anorexia, bulimia, or eating disorder not otherwise specified. EA has also been recognized as central to muscle dysmorphia, the Adonis complex, or bigorexia—common names for reverse anorexia affecting younger men whose distorted self-image and self-esteem demand ever-increasing muscle development.

EA may occasionally be a symptom of body dysmorphic disorder, used to reshape body parts such as the stomach and legs, with which individuals are irrationally obsessed and dissatisfied. Finally, EA exists in pure form apart from these several disorders as an unhealthy use and frequency of exercise driven by body-image issues without disordered eating or body dysmorphia.

Unlike eating disorders, EA does not routinely involve secrecy but more often indifference or failure to recognize the problem, such that it is not discussed during treatment and loved ones may not realize the need for concern. Those with EA often are comfortable with their EA because, unlike other compulsive behaviors such as repetitive checking, EA may be perceived as healthy and socially acceptable.

The Importance of Screening

EA may lead to medical complications: stress fractures, spinal scoliosis [curvature], osteoporosis, loss of menses, heart arrhythmias, and prolonged electrical conduction of the heart with sudden death. Eating disorder patients with EA have greater likelihood of medical decompensation and death than those with more traditional eating disorders. It is therefore critical to screen for EA.

Anyone with disordered eating (especially young men, young and middle-age women, athletes, and any other patient appearing thin or with noticeable muscle tone/development) should be screened for EA with the following questions:

- Do you feel guilty when missing workouts?

- Do you exercise when sick or hurt?

- Would you skip family time, going out with friends, or other obligations to work out?

- Do you panic when missing workouts?

- Do you calculate how much to exercise based on how much you eat?

- Is sitting still problematic because you're not burning enough calories?

- If you cannot exercise, do you feel compelled to reduce what you eat?

"Yes" to one or more of these questions suggests possible EA and should trigger comprehensive evaluation, including gathering objective information about exercise quantity, frequency, and content, as well as patients' subjective experiences of their exercise activity and its connection to their body image and self-esteem. A medical provider should be involved to evaluate EA's often hidden medical consequences. For athletes, it may be useful to collaborate with coaches and families to improve evaluation and formulate congruent goals.

Treating Exercise Addiction

Treatment includes eight factors. Because healthy activity is essential, no more than short-term abstinence from cardiovascular exercise should be recommended. Once patients are medically stable, education and practice in healthy exercise as defined by the American College of Sports Medicine should ensue.

Medical status. Assessing current medical status is critical. This is best done by medical providers experienced with EA and/or eating disorders because of EA's subtle and paradoxical symptoms, which can be misconstrued. Signs of illegal drug, over-the-counter drug, and steroid use should be assessed.

Nutritional status. At a minimum, a one-time assessment with a dietitian is prudent, since many EA patients lack accurate nutrition knowledge, ascribe to nutrition myths/fads, and engage in disordered eating. Follow-up sessions may be needed. Individuals should not participate in exercise or sports until they comply with nutritional recommendations and achieve a medically stable weight as determined by a physician and/or dietitian.

Eating disorder behaviors. Patients with significant eating disorder behaviors are at a high risk of EA relapse and medical complications from the combined eating disorder and EA. Eating disorder behaviors therefore must be reduced before exercise resumption, including normalizing eating, stabilizing weight, and decreasing bingeing/purging. . . .

Body image and self-esteem. All EA cases require body-image and self-esteem interventions. A variety of individual and group techniques exist for addressing body image, both cognitive-behavioral and experiential. Self-esteem work often involves assisting patients to develop a self-concept based on attributes apart from appearance, assertion, and social skills training, and discussion of sex role and sexuality if necessary.

Motivation. Providers should understand patients' motivation for recovery. Individuals with strong internal motivation for change may return to exercise sooner than those who have entered treatment because of external pressures such as parents, schools, or employers. The latter may mask their EA only enough to pacify others.

Cognitions and skills. Cognitive-behavioral approaches are used to help patients change their attitudes toward exercise. Patients need assistance developing adaptive skills to meet needs that exercise has met previously, such as emotion regulation or distress tolerance.

Treatment for Athletes

Athlete-specific issues. Some athletes may choose not to return to their sport because of recovery risks. Those in judged, endurance, and individual sports; lean sports such as dance,

The Danger of Excessive Exercise

Excessive exercise can damage tendons, ligaments, bones, cartilage, and joints, and when minor injuries aren't allowed to heal, they often result in long-term damage. Instead of building muscle, too much exercise actually destroys muscle mass, especially if the body isn't getting enough nutrition, forcing it to break down muscle for energy.

Mary L. Gavin, "Compulsive Exercise,"
KidsHealth.org, November 2007.

cross-country, track and field, and gymnastics; sports with weight categories; and female sports with revealing clothing have greater relapse risk. . . . Because of greater relapse vulnerability and poorer prognosis, recommendations for athletes with these objectively assessed elevated risk factors would likely need to be more conservative at first with a slower return to full activity levels. Especially at higher levels of competition, parents' and coaches' top priority may be athletes' swift return to competition rather than health. Such external pressures must be addressed. Overall, athlete-specific evaluations resemble a balance sheet of strengths and weaknesses culminating in a prudent decision about the return to sport participation and conditions thereof.

Healthy exercise. Once patients are medically stable, education and practice in healthy exercise should begin, perhaps involving an exercise physiologist, athletic trainer, physical therapist, or dietitian skilled in this area. In making recommendations for healthy exercise—including return to professional sports—providers should work to minimize relapse risk and current/future health problems. Recommendations for exercise should be discussed with and agreed upon by patients. A written terms of participation contract between patients and the treatment team and, when appropriate, athletic departments and family, is useful. The contract can include specifics such as medical, nutritional, therapeutic, and behavioral criteria for exercise or continued competition/training. Listing specific logical consequences is encouraged. Examples might include seeing a dietitian to plan solutions or abstaining from training/competition for a delimited time if weight drops below, or exercise frequency/duration exceeds, a certain amount.

Exercise Addiction Threatens Lives

For years, EA has remained below our clinical radar because most EA patients do not recognize EA as a problem and some, such as athletes, appear healthy and functional. Yet EA can have serious, even fatal, long-term effects. When treating groups at risk for EA, it is therefore clinically responsible to screen for EA attitudes and behaviors and to offer or recommend treatment if needed.

> "Tanning indoors is even safer, because unlike exposure to the sun, the environment is controlled. . . . The anticancer benefits of UV exposure . . . far outweigh the risks associated with overexposure."

Tanning Contributes to Health

The Indoor Tanning Association

In the following viewpoint, writers from the Indoor Tanning Association (ITA) argue that receiving sunlight, either naturally or through indoor tanning, provides important health benefits. These benefits include providing an adequate amount of vitamin D, a nutrient that protects against many diseases. Most people in the United State are deficient in vitamin D, according to the ITA, and indoor tanning provides a safe way for people to get adequate vitamin D through UV exposure. The ITA is an organization of indoor tanning manufacturers, distributors, and facility managers.

As you read, consider the following questions:

1. What preventative measures does the ITA report that the medical community embraced in the past to address vitamin D deficiency?

2. About what percent of Americans do not get enough vitamin D, according to the ITA?

3. What illnesses has vitamin D been shown to prevent, according to the ITA?

Sunlight essentially runs our planet, providing:

- energy for plants to grow;

- heat for some animals and reptiles to warm their bodies; and

- essential vitamins for us to live healthy lives.

When ultra violet (UV) light touches our skin, our bodies are able to produce vitamin D. This aptly named "sunshine vitamin" helps strengthen our bones, protect our immune system, and ward off many deadly diseases. Getting a daily dose of UV light—whether it's from the morning sun or a tanning booth—is just as important to our wellbeing as taking the rest of our vitamins. In fact, *Time* magazine named the "benefits of vitamin D" as one of the top 10 medical breakthroughs of 2007.

The Medicinal Properties of UV Light

During the 18th and 19th centuries, American workers began to leave farms for factory jobs. This process of industrialization and urbanization meant that workers and their families spent less time outdoors and, therefore, got less sun exposure. The result? The percentage of the population suffering from vitamin D deficiency soared.

To combat this problem, the medical community embraced several preventive measures such as:

- fortifying certain foods with vitamin D;

- offering vitamin D supplements; and

- exposing individuals to therapeutic UV lamps.

These measures were effective for centuries. But then something changed. Though fortification and supplementation continue to play a role in public health, phototherapy has practically disappeared. On top of that, about 30 years ago, the sunscreen industry launched campaigns, warning the public to avoid *all* UV light by covering up and applying sunscreen, which blocks the body's ability to make vitamin D. As a result, increasing numbers of Americans are (once more) not getting the amount of vitamin D recommended by medical experts. . . .

The quality of sunlight can vary based on geography, pollution, season, and time of day. On the other hand, the light produced by tanning beds is consistent. Tanning beds are carefully manufactured to mimic the sun's rays in the most ideal situation, generating the same UV ratio: 95 percent UVA light and 5 percent UVB. Tanning salons also offer accurate timers and stop controls, so unlike outdoor sunbathing, you are the one in control. Since tanning beds follow this natural formula, they can provide a plausible substitute for sunlight in the winter, when people in many regions do not get enough sun to produce the necessary levels of vitamin D. . . .

No one can regulate the sun. Fortunately, indoor tanning can be controlled—held to the highest standards by health authorities to ensure our safety. The lamps, booths and beds used in tanning salons are considered "medical devices" and, therefore, fall under the jurisdiction of the Food and Drug Administration. Experts in the industry and government work tirelessly to make certain that tanning salons have the best equipment, ensuring the best and safest results for everyone.

Vitamin D Deficiency

According to Harvard researchers, about 60 percent of Americans don't get enough vitamin D. And doctors estimate that the worldwide figure includes more than one billion people. Though certain segments of the population (pregnant woman, infants, elderly, etc.) experience an increased risk, researchers from the Food and Drug Administration report high incidences of vitamin D insufficiency in almost *all* populations. . . .

Vitamin D isn't like other vitamins that you can easily ingest as part of your diet. It is best absorbed through the skin from exposure to UV light. In order to get the amount of vitamin D produced during 20 minutes of sun exposure or 5–7 minutes in a tanning booth, you would need to eat more than 100 eggs. Even foods with added vitamin D, like milk, don't come close to providing the necessary amount.

Roadblocks to adequate sun exposure are everywhere:

- Geography (Cities in latitudes above 37 degrees get less UV light.)

- Fashion (Robes, hats, or clothing with lots of layers keep light from reaching the skin.)

- Work (Late night shifts or very dark environments keep employees from the sun.)

- Cosmetics (Excessive sunscreen or makeup with SPF 15 and higher prevents *all* vitamin D production.)

- Ethnicity (Darker pigments inhibit the body's ability to naturally produce vitamin D.)

All of these factors ensure that individuals are unlikely to obtain much vitamin D from sunlight.

Vitamin D has been shown to prevent many illnesses:

- heart disease

- multiple sclerosis

- tuberculosis

- schizophrenia

- several forms of cancer

- other chronic health problems

It doesn't take much. Even moderate exposure to ultraviolet (UV) light benefits people concerned about vitamin D deficiency and has proven to boost immunity to certain diseases. . . .

Of course, too much of any good thing can be bad. And that holds true for UV light. Overexposure to the sun can burn our skin. However, the healthy approach to tanning is not an all-or-none mentality. It's important to remember that the risks associated with UV light come from "too much" or "too little," but it benefits our health to regularly get a moderate amount.

In addition to the health benefits, tanning in moderation gives people a "boost"—you just feel better. . . .

Melanoma Misinformation

Getting a regular amount of sunlight is healthy, whether it's outdoors or in a sun bed. Moderate exposure to UV light benefits people with vitamin D deficiency and makes people feel good. However, a great deal of misinformation has been spread about the link between Melanoma and *any* amount of UV exposure.

The truth may surprise you:

- Sunburns, not sun tans are linked to melanoma

- Melanoma is most common among those who work indoors, not outside

- Melanoma appears most commonly on body parts not regularly exposed to sun

Safe, moderate exposure does not increase risk of melanoma skin cancer. And tanning indoors is even safer, because unlike exposure to the sun, the environment is controlled. In fact, the anti-cancer benefits of UV exposure highlighted by recent studies far outweigh the risks associated with overexposure.

> *"[A] nationwide survey found evidence of a public-health threat that goes beyond the familiar warnings that tanning may increase the risk of developing wrinkles and skin cancer."*

Tanning Poses Serious Health Risks

Consumers Union of the United States

In the following viewpoint, the Consumers Union of the United States reports on a survey of tanning facilities in 12 cities. The survey reveals that the facilities are not following safe practices but are putting indoor tanners at risk for cataracts, cancer, the suppression of the immune system, and premature aging. In addition, argue the writers, there is evidence that indoor tanning may be habit forming. The Consumers Union of the United States is an expert, independent, nonprofit organization whose stated mission is to provide a safe, just marketplace for consumers. They are the publishers of Consumer Reports *magazine.*

Consumers Union of the United States, "Indoor Tanning: Unsuspected Dangers," *Consumer Reports*, vol. 70, February 2005, pp. 30–33. Copyright © 2005 Consumers Union of US, Inc. Yonkers, NY 10703-1057, a nonprofit organization. Reprinted with permission from the February 2005 issue of Consumer Reports® for educational purposes only. No commercial use or reproduction permitted. www.ConsumerReports.org.

As you read, consider the following questions:

1. During a consumer's first week of tanning, what is the maximum number of visits recommended by the FDA, according to the viewpoint?

2. What are the two most common types of skin cancer?

3. How does the Consumers Union recommend that people under age 60 receive their supply of vitamin D?

Nearly 30 million Americans, including a growing number of teenage girls, are expected to visit a tanning salon this year. Our nationwide survey found evidence of a public-health threat that goes beyond the familiar warnings that tanning may increase the risk of developing wrinkles and skin cancer.

When we called 296 tanning facilities in 12 cities, many not only denied or downplayed the possible risks but also endorsed unsafe practices. Here are the highlights of our investigation:

- Seventy-five percent of the surveyed employees said we could come every day or as often as we liked, even though we called ourselves beginners.

- Nearly 35 percent denied that indoor tanning can cause skin cancer, claimed it doesn't prematurely age the skin, or said both.

- About 6 percent said they permit the dangerous practice of tanning without protective eyewear.

- More than 20 percent said minors, who may face the greatest long-term risks from such exposure to ultraviolet rays, could come without adult consent.

- About half of states in the U.S. have no tanning-parlor regulations, and the existing rules are sometimes minimal and frequently flouted by parlor employees.

- Overall in our six-question survey the employees gave an average of three to four answers that we consider false, questionable, or inadequate. Only 1 percent answered all questions appropriately. If those findings translate into actual practice, many indoor tanners are being exposed to particularly high risk.

The Dangers of Indoor Tanning

Medical groups have long warned about the dangers of indoor tanning. The American Medical Association and the American Academy of Dermatology unsuccessfully petitioned the Food and Drug Administration [FDA] in 1994 to ban cosmetic-tanning equipment.

Three years later, the Federal Trade Commission [FTC] warned the public to beware of advertised claims that "unlike the sun, indoor tanning will not cause skin cancer or skin aging" or that you can "tan indoors with absolutely no harmful side effects."

In February 1999, still under pressure from the medical community, the FDA announced that current recommendations "may allow higher exposures" to UV [ultra violet] radiation "than are necessary." The agency proposed reducing recommended exposures and requiring simpler wording on consumer warnings. But it hasn't yet implemented either of those changes. An FDA spokeswoman told us that "the agency decided to postpone amendment of its standard pending the results of ongoing research and discussions with other organizations."

To make matters worse, only about half of states have any rules for tanning parlors. In some of those states, the regulation is minimal and may not require licensing, inspections, training, record-keeping, or parental consent for minors.

Dangerous Practices

The FTC's warning to the public about false claims on indoor tanning has apparently minimized such false advertising. But potentially dangerous practices and incorrect or questionable ideas persist, many of them pushed by the tanning-facility employees we surveyed.

Beginners can tan every day. Some 67 percent of the employees said we could come for tanning daily; 8 percent more said we could come as often as we want. Virtually every facility offered tanning packages, which encourage frequent tanning. But the FDA recommends no more than three visits during the first week; the frequency after that depends on the particular sun bed and skin type.

Why would anyone want daily tanning sessions? One possible answer: It may be habit-forming.

A small study from Wake Forest University in North Carolina reported in the July 2004 issue of the *Journal of the American Academy of Dermatology* found that people felt significantly more relaxed after lying in a real tanning bed than in a fake tanner that served as a comparison. Based on preliminary evidence that tanning might stimulate secretion of mood-boosting endorphins, the authors of the study speculated that sun beds might have a druglike reinforcing effect.

You don't need protective eyewear. Six percent of the employees gave that dangerous advice. Federal rules require indoor tanning facilities to provide protective eyewear, such as goggles. Exposure to intense UV light can damage the cornea or retina or eventually cause cataracts. Closing your eyes or wearing ordinary sunglasses is not sufficient.

Gentle tanning works for people with very fair skin. About two-thirds of the employees said that our extremely pale-skinned cousin, who burns but never tans outdoors, could come in for tanning or evaluation. But even the National Tanning Training Institute, an industry group, omits people with such vulnerable skin from its chart on skin types in its current training manual. Moreover, people with such skin face especially high risk from UV radiation, research indicates. We

A Growing, but Dangerous, Business

Despite its link to both melanoma and squamous cell carcinoma, indoor tanning is big business. In fact, published reports indicate that the indoor tanning industry has an estimated revenue of $5 billion, a fivefold increase from 1992. The prevalence of indoor tanning among older U.S. teen girls is as high as 40 percent.

Editors of Drug Week,
"Skin Cancer: New Research on Genetic
Changes in Melanoma and Teens' Use of Indoor Tanning
Could Lead to Better Prevention and Treatment Strategies,"
Drug Week, *August 15, 2008.*

don't know how many employees actually meant the feasible alternative, spray-on tanning, since only a small percentage volunteered that option.

Indoor tanning is safer than sunlight. Both UVA and UVB, the main types of ultraviolet radiation, can tan the skin. Some sun beds emit proportionately less of the skin-burning UVB rays than sunlight does, and more UVA rays. But the radiation from other beds today mimics that of sunlight. And whether the lower-UVB beds are any safer than outdoor light is questionable.

Both UVA and UVB rays contribute to skin aging. Further, each can cause potentially cancerous changes in the cells' DNA, both directly and by creating destructive free-radical molecules. Production of melanin, the tanning pigment, generates additional free radicals. Moreover, the radiation from as few as 10 indoor-tanning sessions in 2 weeks can suppress your cancer-fighting immune system, a 2000 study from the Johns Hopkins University School of Medicine found.

Sun-Bed Safety Is Not Justified

Some research suggests that UVA might be somewhat less likely than UVB to cause the direct DNA damage. But the experts we consulted said that any such difference doesn't justify claims about sun-bed safety. In addition, the tanning industry argues that proper use of sun beds doesn't cause sunburns, a potential risk factor for skin cancer. But several epidemiological studies—including at least one that controlled for sunburn history—have tentatively linked indoor tanning with increased risk of melanoma, the deadliest type of skin cancer.

There's less evidence on other skin cancers. But a study from Dartmouth Medical School and elsewhere, published in 2002 in the *Journal of the National Cancer Institute*, found that indoor tanners had substantially increased risks of basal- and squamous-cell carcinoma, the two most common types of skin cancer.

Our consultants say the overall evidence plus ordinary prudence warrants a presumption of probable risk, particularly for people with lighter complexions.

Indoor tanning is carefully controlled. The total LTV [a type of ultraviolet radiation with wave lengths of 280–315 nanometers] intensity of tanning units is about 2 to 6 times greater than in standard sunshine, according to Jeff Nedelman, a spokesman for the Indoor Tanning Association, a trade organization. But length and frequency of exposure, he says, are the key controls in slowly building a tan without burning. That lets customers receive a moderate amount of ultraviolet light based on their skin type and tanning history, he adds.

However, new tanning bulbs emit considerably more radiation than older bulbs, a change that may not be taken into account. Indeed, our survey and other research indicate that sun-bed operators often fail to appropriately control the length and frequency of exposure. A 2003 study from the University of Washington School of Medicine and elsewhere, involving 50 North Carolina tanning facilities and published in the *Jour-*

nal of the American Academy of Dermatology, found that 95 percent of novice tanners were exposed to LTV radiation for a longer time than the federally recommended levels. One-third of them started at or above the maximum exposure limits for already-tanned people.

A study published in 2001 in the same journal by researchers at San Diego State University and elsewhere found that none of 54 facilities in the San Diego area complied with all seven FDA rules and recommendations on length and frequency of indoor tanning; 94 percent allowed more-frequent sessions than the FDA recommends. Both North Carolina and California regulate tanning parlors.

The Age Factor

Moderate tanning won't age your skin. Nearly half of the tanning-facility employees made that claim. (About 18 percent denied that any tanning would cause aging.) It's true that the potential damage rises with increasing exposure to UV radiation. But any tan indicates that your skin has undergone some cellular damage, which is what triggers the melanin production. No one knows how many times you can tan before the damage becomes visible, but it's cumulative and largely irreversible.

Lotions can reduce the aging effects of indoor tanning. Preliminary research suggests that topical lotions containing antioxidant vitamins might possibly reduce skin damage if applied before tanning. But any such protection would be quite minimal, says photobiology expert Vincent DeLeo, M.D., chairman of the dermatology department at St. Luke's-Roosevelt Medical Center and Beth Israel Medical Center in New York. Indeed, Nedelman, spokesman for the tanning association, says the vast majority of products are moisturizers. In 1997 the FTC ordered California Suncare of Los Angeles to stop saying its California Tan Heliotherapy tanning lotions, oils, and gels prevent or minimize skin cancer and premature skin aging. The company complied without admitting any wrongdoing, according to the FTC.

Indoor tanning may help disease. It's true that LTVB stimulates the skin to synthesize vitamin D. And some research suggests that adequate vitamin D may help ward off not only osteoporosis but several other diseases as well, including certain common cancers. But there are safer ways to get enough D.

People under age 60 or so can get a year's supply in most parts of the U.S. by going outdoors for several minutes between midmorning and midafternoon a few times a week during the spring, summer, and fall in the North or any three seasons in the South. Those who are older or heavier, have darker skin, or live farther north need somewhat more exposure. Alternatively, you could regularly eat foods high in vitamin D, notably fortified milk and fatty fish, or take a multivitamin or other pill containing the vitamin.

Periodical Bibliography

The following articles have been selected the supplement the diverse views presented in this chapter.

American Cancer Society   "Cellular Phones," May 28, 2008, www.cancer.org.

Salynn Boyles   "Skin Cancer Researchers Oppose Industry Campaign to Portray Tanning Beds as Healthy," *WebMD Health News*, September 18, 2008, www.webmd.com.

Centers for Disease Control and Prevention, U.S. Department of Health and Human Services   "Physical Activity and Good Nutrition: Essential Elements to Prevent Chronic Diseases and Obesity," 2008, www.cdc.gov.

Amanda Gardner   "Kids with Cell Phones Not As Safe Crossing Streets," *HealthDay News*, April 11, 2008, www.healthfinder.gov.

Tiffany Haufe   "Sun Tanning: Is It Worth the Risk?", *Knight News*, September 25, 2008, www.qcknightnews.com.

Vini Gautam Khurana   "Mobile Phones and Brain Tumours: A Public Health Concern," *Brain-Surgery US*, 2008, www.brain-surgery.us

Sally C. Pipes   "Don't Put Big Brother in Charge of Weigh-Ins," *The Star-Ledger*, January 1, 2008.

Michelle Rainer   "The Brittle Truth: Think You're Too Young To Worry about Osteoporosis?", *W*, November 2006.

Research Report   "Tobacco Addictions," National Institute on Drug Abuse, July 2006, www.drugabuse.gov.

CHAPTER 3

Have New Technologies and Treatments Contributed to Human Health?

Chapter Preface

In the 1960s television series *Star Trek*, Dr. McCoy frequently recalled with horror the medical technology of twentieth-century Earth, wondering how people could have been so barbaric and primitive in their medical knowledge. While Dr. McCoy would probably still be horrified with twenty-first century treatments, medical knowledge and technology has quickly advanced, even in the forty years since the first airing of *Star Trek*.

Today, many surgeries can be conducted laparoscopically, a minimally invasive surgical technique using very thin instruments and a video camera. As a result, patients recover from gall bladder surgery, for example, in a matter of days, rather than weeks. Likewise, athletes needing knee repair can often be on their feet and rehabilitating their legs soon after surgery.

Laser technology is another way medical science has advanced. One use of lasers is to reshape the corneas of people with poor eyesight, often providing them with better than 20/20 vision as a result. Similarly, laser scalpels used in surgery offer doctors a more precise instrument for delicate procedures.

Oddly, some of the newest medical advances are not new at all, but rather are a return to old and abandoned practices long regarded as barbaric. Leeches, for example, were widely used by doctors for centuries. According to Ker Than, in the April 19, 2005, article "Maggots and Leeches: Old Medicine is New," appearing in *LiveScience*, "In ancient times, leeches were used to treat everything from headaches to ear infections to hemorrhoids." George Washington was repeatedly bled, a technique using leeches to extract blood from a patient, by his physicians. Throughout most of the twentieth century, doctors and patients rejected the use of leeches. Recently, however, researchers have discovered that leeches could be used effectively to "drain blood from swollen faces, limbs and digits after reconstructive surgery," according to Than. Because leech saliva prevents blood clotting, leeches are especially useful when doctors must reattach small parts of the body that would die if a blood clot formed. Furthermore, researchers are finding additional uses for leeches, including treatments for arthritis and glaucoma.

Maggot therapy is another old treatment in medical literature, used to remove dead tissue from a wound or burn. As late as the 1940s, maggots were often used to help clean wounds. With the advent of antibiotics to treat infection, the use of maggots was largely abandoned. Now, however, the emergence of antibiotic resistant bacteria requires doctors to be more judicious in the use of antibiotics. Introducing maggots into a patient's wounds allows dead tissue to be removed, healthy tissue to reappear, and the wound to be kept clean of bacteria. In patients with diabetes, for example, who frequently lose limbs to gangrene caused by foot infections, maggots can often clear the gangrene and save the limb.

Clearly, a new treatment is not necessarily beneficial simply because it is new, nor is an old treatment bad just because it is old. The writers of the viewpoints in this chapter take a close look at how new technology and new treatments are affecting modern health care.

> *"The main reason why blockbuster statins work may [be] ... because they reduce the inflammation that leads to heart attacks."*

Statins Can Prevent Cardiovascular Disease

John Carey

In the following viewpoint, John Carey argues that an important study has shown that statins may not only lower cholesterol but also reduce inflammation, thus resulting in fewer heart attacks. He also asserts that cholesterol may not be as important a factor in cardiovascular disease as previously thought and that inflammation could be the real culprit. In either case, statin drugs such as Crestor have empirically demonstrated their value in preventing heart attacks, according to Carey. Carey is a senior correspondent for Business Week.

As you read, consider the following questions:

1. According to national treatment guidelines, everyone's bad cholesterol levels should be at what level?

2. Who is the AstraZeneca chief executive cited in this viewpoint?

3. Why has Dr. Paul Ridker been criticized, according to Carey?

The idea that lowering cholesterol is the key to preventing heart attacks and cardiovascular disease has taken a couple of big hits recently. The first came on Mar. 30, when a panel of cardiologists recommended that Zetia and Vytorin, cholesterol-lowering drugs marketed by a joint venture of Schering-Plough (SGP) and Merck (MRK), be used only as a last resort. The reason: A clinical trial adding Zetia to other cholesterol-reducing drugs had failed to show a benefit [BusinessWeek.com, 3/31/08].

But in the furor over Zetia and Vytorin, an equally dramatic but largely unnoticed development occured the next day. On Mar 31, AstraZeneca (AZN) announced that it was halting early a 15,000-patient trial of its cholesterol-lowering drug, Crestor—because the drug was working better than expected. The surprising twist: When the patients started taking the drug, their "bad" cholesterol levels were already very low—so low, in fact, that drugs normally would not have been recommended or used. Yet patients on the drug had fewer heart attacks than those untreated in the trial, which was dubbed Jupiter, and the benefit showed up much earlier than expected. "It was stunning to have Jupiter stopped so early," says Dr. James Liao, a researcher in the vascular medicine unit of Brigham & Women's Hospital in Cambridge, Mass., the lead research center for the trial. "It suggests a new paradigm. These drugs may be working in ways other than lowering cholesterol."

That's a heretical notion, given the overwhelming message from doctors, companies, and the media that high levels of bad cholesterol can lead to an early grave and must be reduced. According to national treatment guidelines, everyone's LDL [or bad cholesterol] levels should be brought under 130 mg/dL, and in many cases, lowered as close to 100 as possible.

Nonbelievers

Yet there have always been doubters about the almighty importance of cholesterol levels, and there is evidence that LDL may be only a part—and a small part—of the story. Half of all heart attacks and cases of cardiovascular disease occur in people with normal or even low levels of LDL [BusinessWeek, 1/17/08], for instance. And the Zetia trial showed that different types of cholesterol-lowering drugs don't bring the same benefit. In that trial, the additional LDL reduction from adding a second drug, Zetia, to the standard statin-type drug, which works differently in the body, seemed not to help patients.

Dr. Paul Ridker, director of the Center for Cardiovascular Disease Prevention at Brigham & Women's Hospital and a professor of medicine at Harvard University, was one of those who thought something else must be going on. The evidence, he believed, pointed to a major role for inflammation in causing cardiovascular disease. He became a proponent of testing blood for a biological marker of inflammation, called C-reactive protein [CRP]. Could inflammation be a better indicator of risk than cholesterol levels, he wondered? Maybe statins such as Lipitor work, in part, by reducing inflammation.

Ridker convinced AstraZeneca that it was worthwhile for the company to fund a major trial to test the idea. After all, there was little risk and lots of potential gain for the Anglo-Swedish drug maker. Its drug, Crestor, had been late to the cholesterol-lowering game, and it lagged behind other drugs in the same "statin" class, such as Pfizer's (PFE) Lipitor. But if the trial showed that Crestor worked in patients with low cholesterol, then it could reach a wider market than the other statins. Instead of just selling it to people with high cholesterol, it might also be used in those with high CRP or other indications of inflammation even when they had normal or low cholesterol. That's a potential expansion of the market by some 25 million to 30 million Americans. "The trial was originally conceived to see how important a factor inflammation is in cardiovascular disease," explains AstraZeneca Chief Executive David Brennan.

The trial Ridker launched was huge: 15,000 patients with high CRP levels. Their average cholesterol level: 108, which is very low. Half the volunteers got Crestor; half got a placebo. Ridker designed the study so that, if the drug reduced events like heart attacks by 25%, the benefit in those getting the drug would be noticeable in 3 years. "Our expectation was that the trial would take until 2010 or 2011," says Brennan.

Instead, the benefit was so obvious that the trial was stopped in March, more than two years early, so that patients getting the dummy pill could also benefit. Continuing the trial would have been unethical since it would have denied the benefit to those still on the placebo. The company says it will make the actual data public this fall at a scientific meeting. But the effect is surprisingly large. For the reduction in heart attacks to have been seen so early, the benefit in these patients is as high, or higher, than the benefits seen in patients who start with high bad-cholesterol levels. The implication is remarkable: The main reason why blockbuster statins work may not be because they lower cholesterol, but because they reduce the inflammation that leads to heart attacks. "I think statins do work, but maybe not because they lower LDL," says Liao.

Body Chemistry

Liao's own research has proved that statins have other biochemical effects than lowering cholesterol. Most important, they reduce the amount of an enzyme called Rho-kinase. That, in turn, dials back damaging inflammation in arteries. When Liao knocks down the level of Rho-kinase in rats, they don't get heart disease. And in new, still unpublished work, he has showed that simply reducing Rho-kinase in certain immune system cells is enough to reduce heart disease in rats.

How Well Do Statins Work?

Overall, studies find that statins can lower LDL levels from 10 to 60 percent, depending on the drug and dosage used. One landmark study completed in 1994, the Scandinavian Simvastatin Survival Study, found deaths from heart disease plummeted 42 percent, and deaths from all causes 30 percent, over five years in patients with heart disease who took Zocor. Several other studies found that Pravachol reduced heart attacks, surgical bypass, and angioplasties in patients without heart disease by lowering LDL levels. And one study found the drug reduced overall deaths in patients who had had a previous heart attack but who had cholesterol levels that were more or less average for the general population. New statins currently under development can lower LDL levels even more—up to 80 percent in some cases—garnering them the moniker "super statins."

Given their tremendous success, it's no wonder that statins are among the most frequently prescribed drugs in the United States. (Lipitor is prescribed more than any other drug in America.) Approximately 12 million Americans take statins. That's a small fraction of the estimated 36 million that doctors believe are eligible for the drugs based on guidelines set by the National Institutes of Health. In fact, some experts suspect that within a few years, half of all American adults will be taking statins, which some call the "drug of the century."

David L. Katz and Debra L. Gordon,
"Statins: The New Wonder Drugs," Cut Your Cholesterol,
Reader's Digest, 2004.

Depending on details of the data from the Jupiter trial, it may be possible for AstraZeneca to convince the Food & Drug

Administration that Crestor should be approved for people with low cholesterol but high levels of inflammation in their arteries. That could turn the drug, now a $2.7 billion-a-year best-seller, into a mega-blockbuster. Without FDA approval, the company can't yet market the drug for this new use, "but we think it will take the science in a certain direction, towards inflammation," Brennan says. A year's supply of the 20mg Crestor dose used in the Jupiter trial costs just under $1,200 when purchased online. If just 5 million more people went on the drug, that would represent an additional $5.2 billion for AstraZeneca—a nearly 200% boost from current sales. And if 10 million in the potential market expansion of 25 million to 30 million people were to take Crestor, the company would add some $11.8 billion in additional annual sales.

One hurdle, however, is exactly how that inflammation should be measured. CRP is seen as a bit of a blunt instrument, since it varies considerably among people and requires multiple tests to establish a true reading. The body's immune system kicks into high gear at the first sign of injury or disease, be it a head cold or broken bone, and inflammation increases. In addition, Ridker has been criticized for having patented the test for CRP at the same time that he is pushing for more widespread testing—a conflict of interest. Others, such as Liao, believe that other biological substances, such as the Rho-kinase enzyme, might end up being a better marker.

Either way, the Jupiter trial adds to the growing evidence that the American obsession with "bad" cholesterol levels may be misplaced. In the coming years, doctors and patients may become far more concerned with how inflamed our arteries are.

"Super high levels of statins [cholesterol lowering drugs] are immune toxic, cripple your body's natural cancer defense system, and weaken nerves."

Statins Pose Serious Health Risks

Byron Richards

In the following viewpoint, Byron Richards argues that Massachusetts Senator Ted Kennedy's 2008 brain tumor may have been caused by statins, drugs administered to lower high levels of cholesterol. He also asserts that statins interfere with the human immune system and cause cancer, facts covered up by the pharmaceutical industry. In addition, he asserts that statins damage brain cells and, in combination with blood pressure medication, make the nervous system vulnerable to cancer. Richards is a board certified clinical nutritionist and natural health expert.

As you read, consider the following questions:

1. Where did Senator Kennedy have surgery for a blocked carotid artery in October of 2007?

2. Why does Richards assert that Kennedy was "no poster child for health"?

3. According to Richards, what important anti-cancer nutrients are reduced by statins?

Legions of well wishers look on as Senator Ted Kennedy struggles for his life, fighting against one of the most difficult types of brain tumors. Few men have had such an impact on the laws made in the United States. As a powerful member of the Senate HELP [Health, Education, Labor, and Pensions] committee Kennedy has been a primary force shaping almost all health-related legislation for decades. Ironically, it may be the drugs he has so adamantly promoted that are the straw that broke the camel's back, leading to his brain tumor.

Kennedy Receives the Finest Care

Few Americans receive the preferential care given to an important Senator like Kennedy. It is interesting to note what the "finest" care enables a person to receive. He is being treated at Boston's Massachusetts General Hospital, arguably one of the best hospitals in the world—the same place he had surgery for a significantly blocked carotid artery in October of 2007.

Now that the public's attention will be diverted onto treating his cancer problem, not too many are going to explain that the care for his carotid artery problem could be a primary reason for his brain tumor suddenly emerging. Indeed, in Kennedy's situation the fox and the hen house are the same hospital—do you really expect them to take a close look at his situation when such an evaluation is self-incriminating? And on the larger scale such an evaluation could lead to millions of Americans dumping their statin drugs in the trash.

Kennedy is no poster child for health, fitness, or a healthy lifestyle. He is overweight and out of shape and has been for a long time. Eight months ago [September 2007] doctors found his left carotid artery mostly blocked and performed surgery to clean out the plaque. It took many years of abuse to create that problem. In all fairness to his doctors, Kennedy is not a very healthy patient. On the other hand, that is what doctors are for—treating patients who aren't healthy and getting them back to real health.

We know from publicly disclosed information that Kennedy was taking both blood pressure medication and statin drugs to lower cholesterol. We can assume that as part of the "finest medical care" his treatment to lower cholesterol was quite aggressive following his carotid artery surgery—now the "gold standard" of care being pushed on countless Americans. This means lowering cholesterol to abnormally low physiological levels, based on the idea that if a person can't make much cholesterol then it can't form plaque. Virtually no attention is given to the potential risks of starving the cholesterol synthesis system throughout the body—which is the core survival system of any person.

Kennedy was also on blood pressure medication. Most doctors think they have done their patients a real favor when they use enough drugs to get their numbers looking better on paper. Unfortunately, blood pressure medication typically reduces the flow of nutrition and oxygen to your brain, resulting in acid pH and an environment readily suitable for cancer growth. There is a huge difference between having normal blood pressure because you are healthy (meaning blood gets to your head properly) and good blood pressure numbers artificially produced with drugs (meaning blood doesn't get to many areas of your body properly, including your brain). There is no short cut to real health.

Statins and Cancer

Statins cause cancer for a variety of reasons, a fact that is consistently covered up by the 20-billion-dollar-a-year statin industry—with the help of Senators from both sides of the political aisle, like Kennedy, who actively support the Big Pharma agenda. In fact, Big Pharma tries to promote statins as a cancer-protective drug based on the ability of statins to kill

Statins and the Brain

Years ago, when I was a medical student, transient global amnesia was very rare, almost a medical curiosity, and deserving of only a very limited description in most neurology textbooks. Fifty years would go by before I again encountered this obscure affliction, despite the fact that for at least twenty-five years of this time I operated a busy family practice seeing dozens of patients daily. Now, in the past several years, this condition has reached seemingly epidemic proportions in emergency rooms throughout North America and Europe. Emergency room doctors have hauled out their sometimes dusty medical books and looked with wonder from book to patient as they realize they are seeing what, for many, is their first case of transient global amnesia. These confused patients, asking over and over again, "What has happened to me?" or some similar question, are completely unable to remember the doctor's explanation offered only moments before. For every case of this type of temporary amnesia, thousands of cases of lesser forms of memory disturbance such as extreme forgetfulness, disorientation and confusion have also been reported to statin drug researchers. Most of these cases do not make it to the emergency rooms and are, undoubtedly, extensively under reported.

All of these cases are associated with the use of the stronger statin drugs such as Lipitor®, Mevacor®, and Zocor®. Sometimes symptoms begin within weeks of starting medication. In other cases several years might pass before the onset of symptoms. Frequently they have been associated with muscle pain and tenderness, the much more common statin drug side effects. . . .

Duane Graveline, Lipitor, Thief of Memory:
Statin Drugs and the Misguided War on Cholesterol.
Duane Graveline, November 2006, pp. 3–4.

cancer cells in test tubes. They do this in test tubes because they are so toxic. In your body a dose required to kill cancer cells would kill you first.

Statins interfere with normal immune function in multiple ways. They are so effective at suppressing your immune system that they have been researched as immune-suppressing options for organ transplant patients. That is not good news for anyone having to fight the flu or combat cancer.

Statins interfere with core survival systems that are "branches" in the normal production of LDL [low-density lipoproteins] cholesterol. Such interference in health is a major side effect of statins—and widely ignored by prescribing physicians. For example, selenium-containing genes are reduced/blocked by statins, including the production of cellular glutathione—your cell's most important antioxidant that protects against cell mutations that can lead to cancer.

Important anti-cancer nutrients such as vitamin D and coenzyme Q10 are also reduced by statins. And a primary anti-cancer cell-modulating substance known as isoprenoids are reduced by statins. Isoprenoids in fruits, vegetables, and whole grains are the reason eating these foods is associated with less cancer. Blocking your body's natural production of them with statin drugs is not a good idea.

Brain Cells and Statins

Brain cells are weakened by statins, as every brain cell has a naturally higher level of cholesterol in its cell membrane so it can live longer (brain cells do not split and divide like other cells).

Thus, super high levels of statins are immune toxic, cripple your body's natural cancer defense system, and weaken nerves. The longer a person stays on these high doses the worse the problems become—as damage is cumulative and insidiously progressive over time. When combined with blood pressure medication this creates an environment within the nervous system ripe for cancer growth, a fact that simply cannot be denied based on the timing of Kennedy's problems.

When a person develops cancer while taking a statin the statin is never blamed—even though it is an obvious causative agent that cannot possibly be ruled out. The risk for cancer is especially true when cholesterol levels are being suppressed to abnormally low levels that virtually no person who is healthy possesses. The "finest" medical care money can buy enables an individual to be poisoned by statins, and the brightest medical minds on earth don't seem to have a clue what they are actually doing to people such as Senator Kennedy.

"*[An] important risk factor for fractures is treatment failure once osteoporosis is diagnosed. . . . Left untreated, [a woman's] fracture risk increases 2.4 times per year.*"

Osteoporosis Treatments Improve Women's Health

Jonathan Labovitz and Shohreh Sayani

Jonathan Labovitz and Shohreh Sayani argue in the following viewpoint that osteoporosis is a serious threat to women's health and, to a lesser degree, to men's. They assert that failing to seek diagnosis and treatment is dangerous in that it increases the risk of fractures and complications from fractures. The writers outline a variety of treatment options, including vitamin supplementation, exercise, pharmaceutical drugs, hormone therapy, and other options still being studied. They conclude that prevention and early treatment are essential. Labovitz and Sayani are doctors of podiatric medicine at Doctors Hospital in West Covina, California.

Jonathan Labovitz and Shohreh Sayani, "Strategies Mount for Treating Osteoporosis Fractures," *BioMechanics*, vol. 15, March 2008. Copyright © 2008 by CMP Media LLC, 600 Community Drive, Manhasset, NY 11030, USA. Reproduced by permission.

As you read, consider the following questions:

1. How many women and men over age 50 will experience a fracture related to osteoporosis during their lifetimes?

2. What is the reduction in the incidence of hip fractures in women who are active versus the incidence in women who are not active?

3. Although hormone replacement therapy (HRT) significantly reduces the risk of vertebral fractures, why do women frequently discontinue the therapy, according to Labovitz and Sayani?

Osteoporosis is a disease of low bone density and architectural deterioration of bone tissue that causes bones to become more fragile. This often leads to an increase in susceptibility to fractures. Osteoporosis already has affected more than 10 million people in the U.S. and the numbers are growing. More than 1.5 million fractures per year are attributable to osteoporosis, resulting in costs of approximately $18 billion. Significant morbidity and mortality results from complications related to osteoporosis, such as fractures of the hip and spine. The incidence of hip fractures rises exponentially with age.

A Silent Disease

Because the disease process is often silent, initially presenting as a fracture, it is crucial to identify at-risk individuals so they can be targeted for prevention or treatment. Knowledge about the risk factors of osteoporotic fractures has increased within the last decade. . . .

Given this situation, other risk criteria, such as age, weight, medication use, history of previous fracture, and maternal history of fractures, need to be assessed. It is estimated that one in two women and one in eight men over the age of 50 will experience a fracture related to osteoporosis during their lifetime. Eighty percent of osteoporotic fractures involve women, the majority of whom are postmenopausal.

Many risk factors contribute to developing osteoporosis and related fractures. Additional risk factors, which can cause falls that result in fractures, include being visually impaired, having reduced mobility, or suffering from depression.

Fracture risk has been found to be independent of gender, despite the fact that women have a greater risk and incidence of osteoporosis. Men and women with approximately the same bone density have nearly the same fracture risk. Overall, women have more fractures because of their lower bone density. Adjusting for race, it has been found that individuals of African descent have greater bone density in comparison with other races. At the same bone density, they experience about 30% fewer fractures. Asians have fewer fractures than Caucasians, even though their bone density is lower.

Not Treating Osteporosis Is Dangerous

Another important risk factor for fractures is treatment failure once osteoporosis is diagnosed. If a patient continues to be left untreated, her fracture risk increases 2.4 times per year. Hip fractures and vertebral fractures tend to be the most devastating, because of their association with extensive debilitation, hospitalization, and death.

Treating osteoporosis is the optimal approach for preventing fractures. The four goals of treatment are prevention of fracture, attainment of increased bone mass, relief of symptoms of fracture or bone deformity, and enhancement of physical function. Prevention efforts begin with bone mineral density testing to target individuals at greatest risk.

Treatment is started in a tiered fashion, beginning with lifestyle changes that include weight-bearing exercise, dietary supplements of calcium and vitamin D, and fall prevention.

The etiology of bone demineralization is also addressed. Pharmaceutical intervention is then used to improve bone density and decrease fracture risk.

Activity level can greatly influence BMD [bone mineral density]. A 42% reduction in the incidence of hip fracture was observed in women who engage in activity compared with those who are not active. Women should be encouraged to engage in weight-bearing physical activity for at least 30 minutes three times a week. High-intensity activity is recommended, but even activity that is not strenuous can prove beneficial, especially for elderly women who are sedentary.

Smoking cessation is another form of preventive treatment. One study found that tobacco use caused a reduction in estrogen, which leads to increased bone resorption. In the study, women who smoked an average of one pack per day had a deficit in spinal BMD of 2% per decade. By menopause, this deficit is more than half a standard deviation lower than in nonsmokers.

Treatment Options

Two classes of pharmaceutical agents are widely used for treatment. The first category is antiresorptive agents, which function to slow bone turnover and allow bone formation to surpass bone resorption. These agents include calcitonin, hormone replacement therapy, selective estrogen receptor modulators (SERMS) [a type of hormone therapy] and the bisphosphonates.

The other option is to directly stimulate bone formation. Anabolic agents amplify the number of osteoblast precursor cells and stimulate them to differentiate into mature osteoblasts. This leads to a net gain in bone formation. Intermittent parathyroid hormone administration has been shown to increase bone turnover and improve BMD, architectural integrity, and bone stability. . . .

Postmenopausal women, the highest at-risk patient population and the most studied, experience bone loss at an average rate of one to 3% per year. Prophylactic treatments can include hormone replacement therapy, bisphosphonates, vitamin K, calcitonin, and, more recently, intermittent PTH [parathyroid hormone].

Because a multitude of choices are available today, one approach is to treat osteoporosis based on its derivation. Hormone replacement therapy with estrogen and progesterone, etidronate, calcitonin, and vitamin K were found to be effective in the reduction of vertebral fractures in women with postmenopausal osteoporosis in one comparative study. At the two-year follow-up, however, vitamin K and etidronate were found to be the least efficient in reducing the rate of bone loss.

Treating Osteoporosis with Biphosphonate Drugs

The bisphosphenates, including risedronate and alendronate, work by accelerating osteoclastic apoptosis [a process that leads to the death of osteoclasts, cells that destroy bone] and inhibiting osteoclastic recruitment, maturation, and activity. Studies have shown a decrease in the number of osteoclasts after four weeks of alendronate administration. Alendronate has specifically been shown to reduce fracture risk and increase BMD at the lumbar spine and hip.

Long-term treatment with alendronate has shown an 11.4% increase in BMD in the lumbar spine after seven years and a 13.7% increase after 10 years. Reduction of hip and spine fractures in preexisting osteoporosis has also been reported.

Alendronate is also used to maintain bone mass and reduce the risk of fractures in postmenopausal women and to increase bone mass in men. It is also indicated for patients with glucocorticoid-induced osteoporosis and Paget's disease,

The Recipe for Bone Health

The good news is that in the last 15 years, researchers have developed effective new treatments for osteoporosis. They're not a cure, but they can help, especially when you exercise and eat right. . . .

The recipe for bone health is simple:

- get enough calcium and vitamin D, and eat a well-balanced diet

- do weight-bearing and resistance exercises

- don't smoke

- drink alcohol only in moderation

- talk to your doctor or health care provider about your bone health. . . .

The antiresorptives available today include:

- bisphosphonates

- calcitonin

- estrogen therapy and hormone therapy

- selective estrogen receptor modulators

The National Osteoporosis Foundation, Bone Tool Kit, *2007.*

a metabolic bone disease. In long-term studies of patients who had low bone mass, alendronate significantly reduced the development of new vertebral fractures and any symptomatic fractures.

In addition to its role in reducing fracture risk and helping to maintain BMD in postmenopausal women, risedronate is approved for glucocorticoid-induced osteoporosis. Daily administration of the agent has been found to increase BMD in the spine, hip, and wrist.

Treating Osteoporosis with SERMS and Hormone Replacement

Lower bone turnover is achieved through the use of SERMs, which have been found to reduce the risk of vertebral fractures by 35% as well as increase bone density in the spine and femoral neck.

Raloxifene has been shown to decrease bone turnover 30% to 40% and increase BMD by an average of 2% to 3% after three years.

In one clinical trial, raloxifene was shown to decrease vertebral fracture risk by 50% in individuals with no history of fractures and by 34% in those with prior vertebral fracture. However, raloxifene showed no benefit in preventing hip fracture, and its effect on BMD was comparable to other antiresorptive drugs, including alendronate. Tamoxifene was found to decrease the risk of clinical osteoporotic fractures by only 19%.

Hormone replacement therapy [HRT] is another treatment option that has been shown to significantly reduce the risk of vertebral fractures. HRT consists of various estrogen and progesterone combinations. Estrogen inhibits osteoclast function and stimulates osteoblast function via an increase in osteoprotegerin. Progestin prompts osteoblast activity. In a cohort study, Hundrup found that HRT decreased the risk of hip fracture by 30%.

Estradiol, when administered in either 0.3 mg, 0.625 mg, or 1.25 mg doses caused an increase in bone mass in a dose-dependent manner. In addition, HRT showed an increase in bone mass directly proportional to age and years postmenopause. However, the various side effects of HRT, along with an increased risk of breast and ovarian cancer, frequently cause women to discontinue therapy.

The Role of Vitamin D

Vitamin D has been found not only to stimulate bone matrix formation and bone maturation, but to enhance osteoclastic activity and influence the differentiation of bone cell precursors. In addition, vitamin D is essential for intestinal absorption of calcium.

Calcitonin [a hormone that promotes the formation of bone] has been shown to inhibit the function of osteoclasts and to reduce bone resorption. . . . [Researchers] found that treatment of postmenopausal osteoporosis with high doses of vitamin D, moderate doses of salmon calcitonin, and calcium supplementation increased trabecular bone mass and prevented the reduction of cortical bone mass in osteoporosis. Other studies have shown that calcitonin alone increased bone mass for approximately two years, whereas . . . [another study's] results suggest that high vitamin D intake with calcitonin can have prolonged beneficial effects.

Vitamin D levels become depleted as the body ages, and supplementation is imperative to reduce fracture risk. Due to the effect of medications on calcium absorption, BMD can also be reduced. Recommended calcium intake for men and women is 1000 mg/day for those below age 50 and 1200 mg/day for those older than 50. Suggested vitamin D intake for men and women is 400 IU [international units]/day for those between the ages of 51 and 70 and 600 IU/day for those older than 71.

New Treatment Options

Research continues to investigate other treatment options for osteoporosis and preventive approaches to minimize risk of complications secondary to the disease.

Hypercholesterolemia medications (statins) have been found to increase bone formation in rodents by two- to three-fold. They were shown to inhibit bone resorption and stimulate bone formation. . . .

Vibration training is a novel mechanical approach to minimize the risk of osteoporotic fractures. When patients are placed on vibration plates, a signal is emitted that strains bone and simultaneously decreases osteoclast activation on a cellular level. Current studies on vibrational medicine show reduced BMD loss and increased trabecular and cortical bone formation in hormone-challenged rats. High-frequency vibrational plates may increase bone and muscle mass in young women with low BMD. This is important because an increase in muscle mass can add to postural stability and decrease the risk of falling.

Because the incidence of osteoporosis is rising and will continue to rise as the population ages, it is inevitable that every practitioner will, at some time, face a patient with an osteoporotic fracture. A multitude of approaches exist for preventing and treating the disorder. However, commencing this process early is essential in order to reduce the risk, and, ultimately, the prevalence of osteoporotic fractures.

| "Drugs that interfere with normal bone metabolism should be treated with suspicion."

Osteoporosis Drugs Harm Women's Health

Adriane Fugh-Berman and Charlea T. Massion

In the following viewpoint, Adriane Fugh-Berman and Charlea T. Massion argue that bisphosphonates, the most commonly used drugs to treat osteoporosis, a disease that causes bones to thin, may actually cause more fractures in individuals taking the drugs. According to the writers, these drugs interfere with the body's normal bone metabolism. In addition, they assert, bisphosphonate-induced fractures take significantly longer to heal. They urge women to reject drug therapy and choose alternative treatments. Fugh-Berman is a medical doctor who teaches at Georgetown University. Massion is a medical doctor and a co-founder of the American College of Women's Health Physicians.

As you read, consider the following questions:

1. What happens in the natural bone remodeling process, according to this viewpoint?

Adriane Fugh-Berman and Charlea T. Massion, "Bone Breaking Drugs?" *Women's Health Activist*, vol. 33, September-October 2008, p. 11. Copyright © 2008 National Women's Health Network. Reproduced by permission.

2. What is a "transverse" fracture and why are they so scary, according to the writers?

3. What do the writers of this viewpoint recommend for treatment of osteopenia and osteoporosis?

An unusual, very serious leg fracture may be linked to bis-phosphonates, a class of osteoporosis [a dangerous thinning of the bones] drugs that includes alendronate (Fosamax), risedronate (actonel), ibandronate (Boniva), and zoledronic acid (Zometa). While bones seem inert, they actually are active, living tissues that constantly adapt to how you use them. If you exercise, your bones get stronger; if you sit on the couch, the opposite happens. Daily activity causes microfractures in bone. These tiny cracks are repaired in a remodeling process in which cells called "osteoclasts" nibble out a framework, upon which other cells called "osteoblasts" build new bone. Normal bone metabolism is a precise and dynamic choreography between bone formation and bone resorption.

Bisphosphonates increase bone density by causing "apoptosis" of osteoclasts (a polite term for murder on the cellular level) while the osteoblasts continue making new bone. These drugs are very useful for treating osteoporosis (severe bone-thinning) and can decrease fractures among osteoporotic patients. But the drugs have been overpromoted and widely prescribed to women who don't need them. Many women are told they have "osteopenia", a made-up condition that has been a windfall for osteoporosis drug makers.

Osteoporosis Drugs May Weaken Bone

Some researchers are concerned that bisphosphonates' long-term inhibition of osteoclasts actually weakens bones. Without guidance from their osteoclast partners, osteoblasts may lay down bone in uncoordinated ways that create thicker, but less flexible bone. And, normal microfractures that are not repaired by osteoclasts can coalesce, causing actual fractures.

These concerns appear to be well-founded. While most osteoporosis-related hip fractures stem from falls and occur near where the thigh-bone joins the pelvis, there are documented cases of "transverse" fractures, in which the femur breaks straight across. Scarily, most occurred with minimal or no trauma: women who were sitting, standing, or walking suddenly had a leg break. (In some cases, women broke first one leg, then, later, the other.) Many had had pain in the area for weeks or months before the fracture, but this type of weakened bone is not visible on X-ray. (After the bone breaks, these drug-related "transverse" fractures show a specific X-ray pattern.) Most of these patients had been taking alendronate (Fosamax) for more than four years.

These broken legs don't heal normally, either. A physician describing her own experience noted that healing was so slow that she couldn't resume normal activity for two years. The delay makes sense among women taking bisphosphonates: bone remodeling is necessary for both large and small fractures, and stopping a bisphosphonate post-fracture won't necessarily help, as the drug stays in the bones for many years. At a recent national continuing education conference on osteoporosis, audience members asked expert speakers about the dangers of these bisphosphonate-related fractures. Sadly, the lecturers (most of whom have financial ties to osteoporosis drug manufacturers) trivialized the reports, calling them "rare" and "insignificant". (Which just goes to show that industry-funded experts can't be trusted.)

Studies Support the Dangers of Biphosphonates

Our own Medline search turned up two case reports, four case series, and a retrospective review of bisphosphonate-related fractures, involving more than 50 patients. In adverse event reporting, 50 cases is a lot—this volume of reports indicates a likely epidemic of such fractures. (Published adverse

Women Should Hold Off on Osteoporosis Drugs

Studies have shown that most women will lose no more than 7% of their bone mass within the decade after menopause. Bisphosphonates have been shown to replace about 8% of bone within five years, so waiting will cost most women nothing. Counter to just about every other preventive healthcare message out there, when it comes to osteoporosis drugs, it's probably better to hold off. "Wait until the risk gets high enough," says Dr. Bruce Ettinger, adjunct clinical investigator at Kaiser Permanente, Northern California. . . .

This dramatic shift from early prevention to later prevention is an attempt to save healthy women from decades of pill popping to prevent a disease many may well never have. Like all drugs, these have side effects that can include upper gastrointestinal irritation, ulcers of the esophagus, upset stomach, bone pain and skin rash. But what has many people concerned is that the long-term effects are unknown. One sign of potential trouble is that dentists are seeing more jaw disease among women taking bisphosphonates.

Susan Brink, "Treat? Or Wait?"
Los Angeles Times, *September 22, 2008.*

events are like cockroaches: if you find one, there are hundreds more hiding). Most physicians are too busy either to report adverse effects to the Food and Drug Administration (FDA) or write them up for a medical journal. Physicians also may not recognize the fracture's significance, especially when "experts" who are industry shills pooh-pooh any connection.

Almost all reports in the medical literature involved alendronate, the oldest and most widely used bisphosphonate. So far, the newer the bisphosphonate, the fewer number of fractures reported, but that may be because it takes time for reports to surface. There's no reason to assume that other bisphosphonates are safer, as all interfere with bone remodeling. Soon, new classes of drugs will be released that inhibit resorption of bone through other means. But, we believe that interfering with normal bone function is a very bad idea.

Alternate, Safe Treatments

What do we recommend? First, if your bone density study indicates osteopenia, say "no" to any drug therapy, including bisphosphonates. Instead, make sure that you get 1500 mg calcium and 2000 IU [international units] of Vitamin D daily, and perform weight-bearing exercise (done standing up, not in water) for at least 30 minutes, four times weekly. Do exercises that involve your hips and entire spine (e.g., yoga, weightlifting).

Second, if you have osteoporosis, but have never had a fracture that occurs with little or no trauma (called a "fragility fracture"), and have been on a bisphosphonate for five or more years, consider stopping that medication now. One major study found that, over a 10-year period, women who took alendronate for 5 years had the same fracture risk as those who took it for 10 years. Stopping now may allow your bone function to recover and resume repairing microfractures before the whole bone breaks.

If you have osteoporosis and have had one or more osteoporosis-related fractures, you are at high risk for more fractures and may benefit from continued bisphosphonate treatment. On the other hand, if you've had a transverse femur fracture or a non-healing fracture, you should stop using bisphosphonates immediately.

Lastly, don't be seduced by the new osteoporosis drugs soon to be released. They'll doubtlessly be promoted as safe, and it's likely that adverse effects won't show up for some time. Drugs that interfere with normal bone metabolism should be treated with suspicion. When, and if, the benefits are better proven, the risks may be better known also.

> "Widespread adoption of [health infor-
> mation technology] . . . could greatly
> improve health and healthcare in
> America while yielding significant sav-
> ings."

Health Information Technology Can Improve Health Care

Richard Hillestad and James H. Bigelow

In the following viewpoint, researchers from the RAND Corpora-
tion argue that health information technology (HIT) will lead to
significant savings, greater efficiency, increased safety, and better
health. They further assert that the cost of implementing this
technology is small when compared to the savings it will gener-
ate. They detail several obstacles in the way of HIT implementa-
tion, notably that health care providers must pay to implement
HIT and that the implementation will lower their revenue. The
writers urge the government to intervene to remove these barri-
ers. RAND is a non-profit research organization.

Richard Hillestad and James H. Bigelow, "Health Information Technology: Can HIT
Lower Costs and Improve Quality?" Rand Health: Research Highlights, 2005. Copyright
© RAND 2005. Republished with permission of RAND Corporation, conveyed through
Copyright Clearance Center, Inc.

As you read, consider the following questions:

1. How does HIT produce efficiency savings, and what are the potential savings per year?
2. How does HIT help with disease prevention, according to the viewpoint?
3. According to the viewpoint, about what percentage of hospitals and what percentage of physicians' offices have an HIT system (at the time the viewpoint was written)?

The U.S. healthcare system is in trouble. Despite investing over $1.7 trillion annually in healthcare, we are plagued with inefficiency and poor quality. Better information systems could help. Most providers lack the information systems necessary to coordinate a patient's care with other providers, share needed information, monitor compliance with prevention and disease-management guidelines, and measure and improve performance.

Other industries have lowered costs and improved quality through heavy investments in information technology. Could healthcare achieve similar results? RAND [a non-profit research organization] researchers have estimated the potential costs and benefits of widespread adoption of Health Information Technology (HIT). The team also has identified the actions needed to turn potential benefits into actual benefits.

HIT's Potential Includes Significant Savings, Increased Safety, and Better Health

The RAND team drew upon data from a number of sources, including surveys, publications, interviews, and an expert-panel review. The team also analyzed the costs and benefits of information technology in other industries, paying special attention to the factors that enable such technology to succeed. The team then prepared mathematical models to estimate the costs and benefits of HIT implementation in healthcare.

HIT includes a variety of integrated data sources, including patient Electronic Medical Records, Decision Support Systems, and Computerized Physician Order Entry for medications. HIT systems provide timely access to patient information and (if standardized and networked) can communicate health information to other providers, patients, and insurers. Creating and maintaining such systems is complex. However, the benefits can include dramatic efficiency savings, greatly increased safety, and health benefits.

Efficiency savings. Efficiency savings result when the same work is performed with fewer resources. If most hospitals and doctors' offices adopted HIT, the potential efficiency savings for both inpatient and outpatient care could average over $77 billion per year. The largest savings come from reduced hospital stays (a result of increased safety and better scheduling and coordination), reduced nurses' administrative time, and more efficient drug utilization.

Increased safety. Increased safety results largely from the alerts and reminders generated by Computerized Physician Order Entry systems for medications. Such systems provide immediate information to physicians—for example, warning about a potential adverse reaction with the patient's other drugs.

If all hospitals had a HIT system including Computerized Physician Order Entry, around 200,000 adverse drug events could be eliminated each year, at an annual savings of about $1 billion. Most of the savings would be generated by hospitals with more than 100 beds. Patients age 65 or older would account for the majority of avoided adverse drug events.

Health benefits. The team analyzed two kinds of interventions intended to enhance health: disease prevention and chronic-disease management. HIT helps with prevention by scanning patient records for risk factors and by recommending appropriate preventive services, such as vaccinations and screenings. . . .

The Benefits of Health Information

Service	Annual Cost (in millions)	Deaths Avoided Each Year
Influenza vaccination	$134–$327	5,200–11,700
Pneumonia vaccination	$90	15,000–27,000
Breast cancer screening	$1,000–$3,000	2,200–6,600
Cervical cancer screening	$152–$456	553
Colorectal cancer screening	$1,700–$7,200	17,000–38,000

Note: Assumes 100-percent participation of all persons recommended to receive the service by the U.S. Preventive Services Task Force. This assumption is intended to set an upper bound for potential costs and benefits, not to suggest that 100-percent participation is probable.

TAKEN FROM: Rand Health, 2005. www.rand.org.

HIT can also facilitate chronic-disease management. The HIT system can help identify patients in need of tests or other services, and it can ensure consistent recording of results. Patients using remote monitoring systems could transmit their vital signs directly from their homes to their providers, allowing a quick response to potential problems. Effective disease management can reduce the need for hospitalization, thereby both improving health and reducing costs.

Overall Savings Are Large Compared with Costs

Costs include one-time costs for acquiring a HIT system, as well as ongoing maintenance costs. Analysis of other industries indicates that full adoption of new technology requires about 15 years. Because process changes and related benefits take time to develop, net savings are initially low at the start of the 15-year period, but then rise steeply.... These savings are from increased efficiency only; health and safety benefits could double the savings.

Current market conditions place serious obstacles in the way of effective HIT implementation.

- Relatively few providers have access to HIT. Only about 20 to 25 percent of hospitals and 15 to 20 percent of physicians' offices have a HIT system. Small hospitals and hospitals with half or more of their patients on Medicare are less likely to have HIT.

- *Connectivity*—the ability to share information from system to system—is poor. HIT implementation is growing, but there is little sharing of health information between existing systems. There is no market pressure to develop HIT systems that can talk to each other. The piecemeal implementation currently under way may actually create additional barriers to the development of a future standardized system because of the high costs of replacing or converting today's nonstandard systems.

- Finally, one of the most serious barriers is the disconnect between who pays for HIT and who profits from HIT. Patients benefit from better health, and payors benefit from lower costs; however, providers pay in both higher costs to implement HIT and lower revenues after implementation. Hospitals that use HIT to reduce adverse drug events also reduce bed-days—and reduced bed-days mean reduced hospital income.

The Government Should Act Now

Government intervention is needed to overcome market obstacles. RAND's recommended policy options fall into three groups: continue current efforts, accelerate market forces, and subsidize change. All three groups rely on the aggressive use of federal purchasing power to overcome market obstacles. Medicare (the Centers for Medicare and Medicaid Service—CMS) is the nation's payment policy leader, the party with the most to gain from HIT's cost and health benefits, and the health-care system's largest payor. CMS's leadership would send strong market signals for adoption.

Continue current efforts. Actions include: Continue support for the development of uniform standards, common frameworks, HIT certification processes, common performance metrics, and supporting technology and structures. To help allay fears regarding confidentiality, expand liability protection for hospitals using HIT and for providers who comply with federal privacy regulations while using HIT networks. Promote hospital-doctor connectivity by allowing hospitals to subsidize portable, standardized HIT systems for doctors (which would require relaxing the current laws that prohibit such subsidies). These actions call for little or no new federal funding.

Accelerate market forces. Develop targeted investments and incentives to promote HIT. Set up a pay-for-use program for those providers using certified, interoperable HIT systems. Additional actions include: Create a national performance-reporting infrastructure to receive and report comparative performance data. Fund research on pay-for-performance incentives. Educate consumers about the value of HIT in improving their ability to manage their own health.

These actions require a moderate initial investment in policy and infrastructure development, with larger investments in later years. For example, pay-for-use programs, which are relatively easy to implement, could be followed by broad-based pay-for-performance programs, which require substantially more development.

Subsidize change. Direct subsidies would greatly speed HIT adoption. Subsidies may be particularly important in overcoming barriers to network development. Actions include: Institute grants to encourage the development of organizations, tools, and best practices to help HIT succeed. Make direct subsidies to help selected providers acquire HIT. Extend loans to support the start-up and early operation of HIT networks.

Convincing individual physicians and their patients of the value and safety of networking confidential data will be critical. Overcoming these challenges requires ongoing investment in framework, standards, and policy development.

Widespread adoption of HIT and related technologies, applied correctly, could greatly improve health and healthcare in America while yielding significant savings. A range of policy options could be used to speed the development of HIT benefits. Government action is needed; without such action, it may be impossible to overcome market obstacles. Our findings strongly suggest that it is time for government and other payors to aggressively promote the adoption of effective Health Information Technology.

| "Electronic records present a massive threat to privacy—health records in particular."

Health Information Technology Can Lead to Loss of Patient Privacy

Deborah C. Peel

The following viewpoint is excerpted from an interview with Deborah C. Peel, a medical doctor and the founder of Patient Privacy Rights, a non-profit organization dedicated to protecting the confidentiality of health records. Peel argues that the movement toward health information technology (HIT) will harm patient privacy. She asserts that the health industry has never done a good job at securing digital records. Further, she accuses corporations of data mining patient records without informed consent from the patients and argues that people have no legal recourse to protect their records.

Deborah C. Peel, "Strengthen Health Information Privacy," *Healthcare Financial Management*, vol. 61, November 2007. Copyright © 2007 by the Healthcare Financial Management Association. All rights reserved. Reprinted by permission from *hfm* Magazine, November 2007, page(s) 32–36.

As you read, consider the following questions:

1. What does Peel predict will happen if all the digital health records in the United States are wired together with no patient control of access?

2. How do individuals who want to get treatment for mental illness privately and off the grid secure their treatment?

3. How many complaints, convictions, fines, and penalties have been levied on corporations who data mine and use patient health information without informed consent?

When the Health Insurance Portability and Accountability Act [HIPAA] was enacted, Congress mandated that the Secretary of Health and Human Services (HHS) issue patient privacy protections. President [George W.] Bush implemented the original HIPAA privacy rule in 2001. The privacy rule established rules and limits on who can use and disclose patients' protected health information. For the first time, it granted patients a federal right to medical privacy. In 2002, the HIPAA privacy rule was amended and every American's right to consent to the disclosure of their protected health information was eliminated. Now, with the HHS Health Information Technology Initiative, the federal government is pushing for wide-scale implementation of interoperable [software from different companies that will work together easily] health IT (HIT).

Some industry experts feel the privacy rule doesn't go far enough in protecting patients' privacy rights and that interoperable HIT will do more harm than good in terms of patient privacy. Deborah Peel, MD, a practicing physician and privacy rights activist, is advocating for restoring the right of consent, the right to health information privacy, which has been the ethical and legal standard for health care for more than 2,400 years. As founder and chairman of Patient Privacy Rights, she has testified at the federal and state levels and presents at national meetings and congressional briefings for the right of patients to control access to their medical records. She recently shared her thoughts on patient privacy.

A Patient Privacy Advocate

Healthcare Financial Management: How did you become involved in advocating for patients privacy rights?

Deborah C. Peel: I first learned about the problems created by the lack of privacy from my patients when I went into practice in the late 1970s. People paid me cash on the barrelhead because they had lost a job or their reputation had been ruined when someone besides their doctor learned they had depression or a substance abuse problem. They were unwilling to get treatment at all unless they knew that no one would find out about it. Since then, I have heard nothing but sad stories of how lives and careers are wrecked when people learn about sensitive mental illness diagnoses. Many people will simply stay "off the grid" and pay cash so that others do not judge them based on fears about their illnesses. . . .

In 2004, I founded Patient Privacy Rights to educate and empower Americans to preserve and protect their fundamental human and civil rights to medical privacy. By then, it was clear that the nation needed an advocacy organization focused on restoring consent; only consumers should control access to their personal health information (PHI)—no one else.

In December 2006. we got the first front-page story on the elimination of health privacy in the *Wall Street Journal*—the victim came to us through our web site.

What do you see as the biggest challenge to protecting patients' privacy in the information age?

Electronic records present a massive threat to privacy—health records in particular. The health system has the most abysmal track record of any industry in the United States for ensuring that digital records are secure. (Two passwords and unencrypted data at rest are the standard "protections.") The healthcare industry has not bothered to invest in state-of-the-art security. Then combine that with the total lack of patient control, and we have a prescription for disaster. If we wire together all the digital records in the United States with no patient control of access, we will see data theft on a scale you cannot believe. It will result in massive fraud in the healthcare system (billing for people who are not real patients or for treatment that did not occur), massive identity theft (health records contain demographic and financial data, too), and violation of people's privacy. The problem with allowing the use of the nation's health data by more than 4 million covered entities, their millions of business associates, and even banks and financial institutions is that too many people will see *your* sensitive records. Once your records are exposed, like Paris Hilton's sex video, they will live for millennia on the Internet. Digital privacy cannot ever be restored, unlike identity theft, which can eventually be fixed.

The challenge is to use "smart" technology, which already exists, to restore consumer control over all electronic PHI in systems architecture and code and to pass "smart" federal legislation. Congress must restore our rights to health information privacy. "Smart" technology includes independent health record trusts (imagine a safe place to keep records that has a fiduciary duty *only* to those who store their data there) and independent consent management tools (so that every data source has to check with your electronic consent tools before doing anything with your data). Consent management tools allow you to change who can see and use your records instantly, block out data down the single data field, and keep complete audit trails of every disclosure.

How to Safeguard Patient Privacy

The Bush administration is strongly encouraging healthcare providers to adopt interoperable HIT [HIT that is universally com-

patible among all health care providers]. The use of HIT is touted as a way to prevent medical errors, increase administrative efficiency, and reduce healthcare costs. These objectives are important to healthcare delivery. How can these objectives be achieved while safeguarding patient privacy?

What has been so misleading is the portrayal of privacy and the right of consent as somehow obstructing health information exchange and HIT; the truth is exactly the opposite. I can tell you as a practicing doctor, it is "consent" that enables people to walk in the door. People just will not seek care if they think their treatment records will be used to discriminate against them in jobs, insurance, education, and credit. It's false to claim that privacy is an impediment to HIT; it actually is the enabler of HIT.

Baking ironclad privacy protections into HIT systems up front is the *only* way the public will ever trust the health system enough to participate. If we don't have privacy and trust, we won't get the data for all the great uses that can be made of it.

The best example is my field, mental health. I would guess more than one-third of those with mental illnesses who get treatment do so entirely privately and off the grid. They pay privately for care, or they attend Alcoholics Anonymous or Narcotics Anonymous for treatment. So what sort of data do you suppose we have for mental illnesses? Bad data, incomplete data, erroneous data. The avoidance of treatment that is not private will continue to grow because Americans are increasingly realizing that they have no control over access to their health and prescription records in today's health system.

Polls show those with chronic illnesses and those with stigmatized illnesses are the most afraid for their privacy in electronic systems. Pardon me, but aren't those exactly the groups that we want to get treated?

This administration [of George W. Bush] has systematically attacked health privacy rights: first by gutting the HIPAA privacy rule in 2002; then by illegally delegating the determination of the nation's rights to health privacy to unelected bureaucrats and industry appointees to the American Health Information Community, the Certification Commission for Healthcare Information Technology, the Health Information Technology Standards Panel, and more; and then by issuing Executive Orders to eliminate health privacy rights, rather than letting Congress deliberate and write laws. . . .

Improving Safeguards

Do you feel enforcement of HIPAA's provisions has been carried out effectively? What would you recommend as improvements to this process?

There is no meaningful enforcement, as you know; there have been more than 27,000 complaints filed and just a handful of convictions for identity theft, and no fines or penalties have been levied on the corporations that data mine and use our PHI without informed consent. This administration will not punish the real offenders—those who behave as if HIPAA is the law of the land (the rule essentially legalized data mining). The problem is that HIPAA also says that stronger state laws and medical ethics are supposed to prevail; HIPAA was intended to be a floor of protections, not a ceiling. But those designing health IT systems have ignored the strong privacy rights and protections that the public has in the laws of all 50 states, common law, constitutional law, tort law, the physician-patient privilege, the psychotherapist-patient privilege, and as embodied in the medical ethics derived from the Oath of Hippocrates [which encourages care givers to act in the best interests of the patients].

But the biggest problem is that since HIPAA was gutted, there is nothing to enforce! About 70 percent of the complaints were dismissed because there were no violations of HIPAA now that individuals cannot control who can see and use their medical and prescription records. . . .

What role do you think healthcare financial executives can and should play in the public policy debate over HIT and patient privacy?

The public has to tell Congress to end the rampant theft and misuse of the most sensitive data on earth: our PHI. Every poll shows this is what all Americans want—privacy enjoys strong bipartisan support.

Healthcare financial executives should understand how important privacy is to the public and make sure their institutions are not violating privacy. Stronger state laws and medical ethics should prevail. Executives should defend the longstanding rights Americans have had since the founding of the nation to decide who can see and use their health information. They should look at their institution's practices around privacy and security and not sign any IT vendor contracts that give the vendor ownership or rights to access and use patient data. Hospital executives should end the practice of selling hospital data sets and also understand that health data can never be de-identified (the data are too rich with details such as places, dates, and tests to ever have all these unique identifying pieces of information "scrubbed" out of the records), so selling or sharing data sets that are supposedly anonymous or de-identified risks privacy violations that they or the institutions they work for will be liable for. Executives should invest in state-of-the-art security systems, because industry standards are abysmal.

Periodical Bibliography

The following articles have been selected to supplement the diverse views presented in this chapter.

Joseph Conn

"In the Interest of Privacy," *Modern Healthcare*, Vol. 37, No. 20, May 14, 2007.

Danna Cotner and Randal Begley

"Biophosphonate-associated Necrosis of the Jaw," *WDJ: Woman Dentist Journal*, March 28, 2007, www.wdjournal.com.

Christopher W. Hansen

"Embrace Digital Health Data," *The Press-Enterprise*, April 5, 2008, www.pe.com.

Jenny Hope

"HRT Helps Insomnia, Aching Joints and Sex-Life in Women—Even Years after the Menopause, Say Scientists," *Mail Online*, August 22, 2008, www.dailymail.com.

Alan Horwitz

"Fosamax and Its Consequences—Drug May Result in Countless Lawsuits," *Medical News Today*, January 22, 2007, www.medicalnewstoday.com.

Anna Wilde Mathews

"When a Mammogram Isn't Enough," *Wall Street Journal Online*, June 24, 2008, online.wsj.com.

Deven McGraw

"Comprehensive Privacy and Security: Critical for Health Information and Privacy," Center for Democracy and Technology, May 2008, www.cdt.org.

Tanya Harter Pierce

"Mammograms: Are They Safe? Are They Effective?" *Outsmart Your Cancer*, 2008, www.outsmartyourcancer.com.

Jason Tirotta

"Case Western Reserve University Professors Call for Regulation of Electronic Health Records," Press Release, Case Western Reserve University, October 30, 2008, www.eurekalert.org.

**OPPOSING
VIEWPOINTS®
SERIES**

CHAPTER 4

Does America's Health Care System Contribute to Human Health?

Chapter Preface

The American health care system offers some of the finest medical treatment available in the entire world. People travel from across the globe, for example, to visit the specialists at the Mayo Clinic in Rochester, Minnesota, or those at Harvard Medical Center in Cambridge, Massachusetts. In addition, Americans are living longer now than ever before, and people who would have previously died from their ailments have found new and better treatments that allow them to survive longer.

Nevertheless, although the United States prides itself on being a nation where people are treated equally, without regard to race, ethnic background, age or gender, many people contend that American health care has evolved into a system of great inequity, with different standards of care for the rich and the poor, and differing survival rates for the majority and minority cultures. In addition, an increasing number of Americans are finding themselves in the ranks of the uninsured, rendering them more vulnerable to inadequate health care.

According to the 2006 pamphlet "Addressing Racial and Ethnic Health Care Disparities," published by the Institute of Medicine of the National Academies, minorities are less likely to receive kidney dialysis, the most recent treatments for cancer or stroke, the best therapies for AIDS, and the best treatment by medical staff when compared with whites. In addition, the same source reports that "mortality rates for black babies remain [in 2006] nearly two-and-one-half higher than for whites, [and] life expectancy for black men and women remains at nearly one decade fewer years of life compared with their white counterparts."

The American Medical Association reported in a 2009 article, "Eliminating Health Disparities," that recent studies have shown that despite the steady improvements in the overall health of the United States, racial and ethnic minorities experience a lower quality of health services and are less likely to receive routine medical procedures and have higher rates of morbidity and mortality than non-minorities. Disparities in health care exist even when controlling for gender, condition, age and socio-economic status.

The Centers for Disease Control and Prevention (CDC) statistically confirms the gap between majority and minority cultures with regard to health and health care. According to 2008 CDC data, American Indian and Alaska natives have 1.4 times the infant mortality rate as whites, for example. American Indian and Alaska Native babies are also twice as likely as white babies to die from sudden infant death syndrome.

Disparity in health care is not limited to the differences between majority and minority cultures, however. There is also a marked difference between the care received by financially secure people and those who are economically disadvantaged, largely due to the system of health insurance most common in the United States. Traditionally, most Americans have received health insurance through their employment. However, recent trends suggest that fewer employers are offering health care, and those that do are requiring employees to pay higher premiums. For the most part, workers clustered in low-paying full-time or part-time jobs are not likely to have health insurance benefits. Even if health insurance is offered at the place of employment, those workers who have a relatively low income are often unable to afford the high cost of insurance premiums, leaving them uninsured. The National Coalition on Health Care (NCHC) reports that in 2007, fewer people held employment-based health insurance than at any time in the previous ten years. In addition, the NCHC argues that "lack of insurance compromises the health of the uninsured because they receive less preventative care, are diagnosed at more advanced disease stages, and once diagnosed, tend to receive less therapeutic care and have higher mortality rates than insured individuals."

The problem of providing adequate and timely health care for all Americans is a difficult one, and one that is beset by issues of race, age, gender, and socio-economics. The writers of the viewpoints in this chapter look at the American health care system from many perspectives, including the disparity of treatment.

> *"By giving more Americans more control over their health care decisions . . . we will preserve the system of private medicine that has made our nation's hospitals and health care the best in the world."*

America Has the Best Health Care System in the World

George W. Bush

In the following viewpoint, excerpted from a speech to the American Hospital Administrators, former U.S. President George W. Bush argues that America has the best health care system in the world. He asserts that either the government makes health decisions for people, or people make their own decisions with their doctors' help. Then he outlines his administration's commitments to health care, notably the changes in Medicare and Medicaid, the establishment of community health centers, the establishment of health savings accounts, and the movement toward health information technology. He pledges to preserve the private medicine system in the United States.

George W. Bush, "President Discusses Health Care Initiatives," WhiteHouse.gov, May 1, 2006.

As you read, consider the following questions:

1. What former U.S. President signed the bill establishing Medicare over forty years ago?

2. How many new or expanded health care centers did the government fund between the time President Bush took office and the time of his speech to the American Hospital Association?

3. What is President Bush's fifth policy to confront the high cost of health care?

America has the best health care system in the world, pure and simple. We got the best medicines, we got the best doctors, and we have the best hospitals. And we intend to keep it that way. Yet, we are challenged by the fact that health care costs are rising sharply. In the past five years, private health insurance premiums have risen 73 percent. And as a result, some businesses have been forced to drop health care coverage for their employees. You [members of the American Hospital Association] know that as well as anybody. Others have been forced to raise co-payments and premiums. Some have been paying increasing health care costs and, therefore, have been unable to give workers the pay raises they need to cope with rising health care costs.

With rising costs, many Americans are concerned. They're concerned they're not going to be able to afford health care. As you well know, millions of our fellow citizens have no health insurance at all. And as you know, that places burdens on our nation's hospitals. This is unacceptable for this country to have health care costs rising as fast as they are. If we want to be the leader of the world, we must do something about it. And my administration is determined to do something about it.

Two Competing Philosophies

To make our health care system work for all Americans, we have to choose between two philosophies: one that trusts government to make the best decisions for the people's health care, or one that trusts the people and their doctor to make the best decisions for their health care.

We know from experience which of these systems works best. Other nations that have opted for bigger government and more centralized control now have long waits for treatment for the people. The quality of care is lower. There's less technological innovation. In America, as you know, we follow a different path. We lead the world in health care because we believe in a system of private medicine that encourages innovation and change.

And the best way to reform this health care system is to preserve the system of private medicine, to strengthen the relationship between doctors and patients, and make the benefits of private medicine more affordable and accessible for all our citizens.

Government has a role to play. Don't get me wrong. We're ... big in the health care field, as you may know. We have a major role to play in strengthening and reforming this health care system, but in a way that preserves the doctor-patient relationship.

The Health Care Strategy of the Bush Administration

And that's what I want to talk to you about today. The first goal of our health care strategy is to meet the obligation the federal government has made to take care of the elderly and the poor. We have said, as a federal government, we will help the elderly and the poor. And I intend to keep that obligation. We're meeting that obligation, that responsibility through Medicare, Medicaid, and community health centers.

More than four decades ago, the federal government established Medicare to provide health coverage for older Americans. The bill was signed by Lyndon Baines Johnson. He came from a state I know pretty well [Texas]. When I came into of-

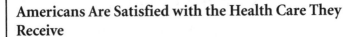

Americans Are Satisfied with the Health Care They Receive

Respondents answered the following question:
Overall, how would you rate the quality of health care you receive— as excellent, good, only fair, or poor?

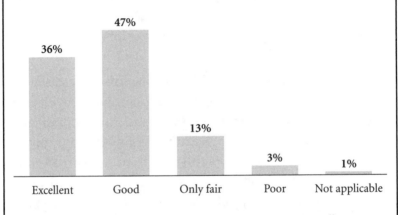

Excellent	Good	Only fair	Poor	Not applicable
36%	47%	13%	3%	1%

TAKEN FROM: Gallup Poll, November 13–16, 2008. www.gallup.com.

fice I found a Medicare program that was outdated, a Medicare program that was not meeting the needs of America's seniors. The way I tried to explain it to the American people was this: We had a system that would pay $28,000 for an ulcer surgery, but not the $500 it would cost for prescription drugs that would prevent the ulcer from . . . taking hold in the first place. And that didn't make any sense—$28,000 for the surgery, but not a dime of prescription drugs to prevent the surgery from being needed. To me that's an outdated system. It's one that's not very cost-effective, and it's one that does not provide quality care for our seniors.

So I decided to do something about it. And I worked with the Congress, and we passed critical legislation that modernizes Medicare and provides seniors with more choices to the private sector, and has given our seniors better access to the prescription drugs they need. . . .

The Government's Commitments

We're honoring our nation's commitments to take care of the poor by strengthening Medicaid. Medicaid is a program administered in conjunction with the states that provides health care for low-income families with children, poor seniors, and disabled Americans. To help improve Medicaid, earlier this year, I signed legislation to restructure Medicaid and give states more flexibility in designing better programs to cover their citizens.

Under the reforms I signed into law, it's now easier for states to offer alternative benefit plans, provide coverage to more people, and design their Medicaid program to meet their state's needs and budgets. In the coming months, my administration will be encouraging states to adopt common-sense reforms. Our health care system must be guided by the needs of patients, not by rules emanating out of Washington, D.C.

Another way we're meeting our commitment to Americans in need is through community health centers. These centers provide primary health care for the poor, so they don't have to go to the emergency room of a hospital to get routine care. This is a really good use of taxpayers' money. It makes a lot of sense to have community health centers so that we can cut down on unnecessary visits to the emergency rooms. Health centers help lower the cost of health care for everyone.

Since I took office we've funded about 800 new or expanded health centers, bringing our total to more than 3,700 health centers serving more than 13 million Americans a year. And over the next two years, we will fund the opening and expanding of 400 more health centers. And Congress needs to fully support these health centers in the budget that I have submitted.

And so we have got a strategy to ... help our elderly and the poor and the disabled. But the second part of our strategy is to make care and coverage more affordable and available for Americans. And here are five key policies to support this goal.

Our first policy is to expand health savings accounts [HSAs] to help improve health care and to help lower costs. Under the current system, as you well know, most Americans have no idea what the actual cost of their treatment is. Third-party insurers pay their bills. So patients have no reason to demand better prices, and the health care industry is under little pressure to lower prices. When somebody else pays the bills, it seems like everything is just fine. The result is that health care costs are skyrocketing. The insurance companies pass these rising costs on to their workers, on to workers and their employees in the form of higher premiums.

Now, health savings accounts transform what I believe is an outdated system by putting patients in control of how their health care dollars are spent. And when patients and consumers see how their health care dollars are spent, they demand more value for their money. The result is better treatment at lower costs. . . .

Transparency in American Health Care

The second policy for making health-care more affordable and accessible is to increase transparency in our health care system. To be smart consumers, we need to be informed consumers, and this is especially true for patients with HSAs who have an incentive to spend their HSA dollars wisely. They need to know in advance what their medical options are, the quality and expertise of the docs and the hospitals in the area in which they live, and what their medical procedures will cost.

My administration is working with the AHA [American Hospital Association] and other health care associations to provide patients with reliable information about prices and quality on the most common medical procedures. And I want to thank the AHA board for adopting a resolution this week supporting transparency. I appreciate your leadership on this vital issue.

We must work together to get patients the information they need so they can get the best quality care for the best price. If you're worried about increasing costs, it makes sense to have price options available for patients. That's what happens in a lot of our society; it should happen in health care, as well. By increasing transparency, the idea is to empower consumers to find value for their dollars and to help patients find better care and to help transform this system of ours to make sure America remains the leader in health care....

The third policy is to provide modern information technology to our medical system. Too many doctors' offices and hospitals have the most advanced technology in the 21st century, but still use last century's filing systems. Doctors are still writing out files by hand. And that's kind of dangerous because most doctors don't write too well. In hospitals, there's more risk of medical error and duplicate tests when records are handwritten on paper instead of cross-checked on a computer....

Health Care at a Discount

The fourth policy is to make it easier for small businesses to obtain the same discounts the big companies get when obtaining health care insurance. Unlike big businesses, small companies cannot negotiate lower health insurance rates because they can't spread their risk over a larger pool of employees. So we proposed association health plans that will allow small firms to band together across state lines and buy insurance at the same discounts available to big companies. The House has passed a bill. The Senate hasn't acted, and now it's time for the United States Senate to do something good for the small business employers of this country.

Our fifth policy to confront high cost health care and to make sure private medicine is central in the United States is to confront the glut of frivolous lawsuits that are driving good doctors out of practice and driving up the cost of health care.

To avoid junk lawsuits, professionals in the health care field are forced to practice defensive medicine. They order tests and write prescriptions that are not necessary, so they can protect themselves from trial lawyer lawsuits. One hospital CEO [chief executive officer] in New York said, "Fear of liability does nothing but threaten patient safety by discouraging open discussion of medical errors and ways to prevent them."

The story of America's hospitals is a story of America's commitment to be a nation of care and compassion. America's strength and its goodness and prosperity is built on a trust in the extraordinary wisdom and power of the American people. And so I believe that by giving more Americans more control over their health care decisions, we will strengthen the doctor-patient relationship, and we will preserve the system of private medicine that has made our nation's hospitals and health care the best in the world.

> *"We spend the most on our health care . . . and our health system is mediocre-to-poor, with 47 million of us lacking the insurance necessary to easily access it."*

America Does Not Have the Best Health Care System in the World

Ezra Klein

In the following viewpoint, Ezra Klein uses data from a survey conducted by the Commonwealth Fund to argue that the American health care system is bad. He asserts that Americans spend twice as much as any other nation, doctors are not paid according to their quality, many Americans cannot even access health care because of a lack of insurance, and many do not have a regular physician. In addition, Klein argues, U.S. citizens have many chronic diseases that are not being treated well. Finally, many Americans are not happy with the current state of health care. Klein is an associate editor of The American Prospect.

As you read, consider the following questions:

1. What percentage of Americans in 2007 did not visit the doctor when they were sick because they could not afford it?

2. What statistics does Klein offer in support of his argument that health care in the United States is not particularly convenient?

3. People of what two countries were most likely to report that they had experienced a medical, medication, or lab error in 2007?

How good is American health care? The developed world is full of alternative models, fully functioning structures that can be viewed as little experiments, the outcomes of which should inform our policies. If our system outperforms its competitors, than we should amplify what sets us apart and pushes us ahead. If we under-perform, we should take a hard look at whether our model really is superior. And luckily, we have the data.

Indeed, we have brand new data. The Commonwealth Fund [a private foundation supporting research on health care issues] just released [in 2007] a broad survey collecting health care attitudes and experiences from patients in Australia, Canada, Germany, the Netherlands, New Zealand, the United Kingdom, and the United States. Here are summaries of some of the findings:

We spend the most. We spend more than any other country in the world. In 2005, our per capita—so, per person—spending was $6,697. The next highest in the study was Canada, at $3,326. And remember—that's "mean" spending, so it's the amount we spend divided by our population. But unlike in Canada, about 16 percent of our population *doesn't have insurance,* and so often can't use the system. These facts should set the stage for all numbers that come after: Every time you see a data point in which were dead last, or not leading the pack, remember that we spend *twice* as much as any of our competitors.

We don't pay doctors according to the quality of their care. One of the first questions is "percent of primary care practices with financial incentives for quality"—in other words, how many doctors are paid, in part, according to the quality of the care they deliver. In the United Kingdom, the number is 95 percent. In Australia, it's 72 percent. The U.S. scores lower than anyone else, at 30 percent. Similarly, electronic medical records—which both increase the quality of care and lower its cost—have 89 percent penetration in the U.K., 79 percent in Australia, 98 percent in the Netherlands, and 28 percent in America. On both these metrics, we perform miserably.

Many Americans Receive No Health Care

Our wait times are low because many of us aren't getting care at all. It's true, Americans do have short waits for non-elective surgeries. Only 4 percent of us wait more than six months. That's more than in Germany and the Netherlands, but considerably less than the Canadians (14 percent) or the Britons (15 percent). But our high performance on the waiting times only accounts for individuals who *get* the care they need. Our advantage dissipates when you see the next question, which asks how many patients skip care due to cost. And here, America is far worse than anywhere else.

In just the past year [2007], a full 25 percent of us didn't visit the doctor when sick because we couldn't afford it. Twenty-three percent skipped a test, treatment, or follow-up recommended by a doctor. Another 23 percent didn't fill a prescription. No other country is even close to this sort of income-based rationing. In Canada, only 4 percent skipped a doctor's visit, and only 5 percent skipped care. In the U.K., those numbers are 2 percent and 3 percent. Few of our countrymen are waiting for the care they need, that much is true.

But that doesn't mean they're getting it quickly. Rather, about a quarter of us *aren't getting it at all.*

Indeed, 19 percent of Americans were unable, or had serious problems, paying medical bills in the last year. Comparatively, no other country was even in the double digits. This is part of why we perform well on the waiting-times metric. In other countries, the disadvantaged wait longer for their care, and so show up in the data tracking wait times. In our country, they disappear from that measure, because they never get the care at all. You don't wait for what you're not receiving. So their wait times show up as "zero," when they should really be something akin to infinite. And would you prefer to wait four months for your surgery, or never get it at all?

Most of us don't have a regular physician. One might expect, given what we pay, that our care would at least be more central and convenient. But it's not so. Of everyone surveyed, Americans were the least likely to report a doctor or general practitioner they routinely saw. As a result, Americans are the most likely to say their doctor doesn't know important information about their medical history, which has obvious implications for care quality, medical errors, etc.

Our care isn't particularly convenient. Nor is medical service more convenient for Americans to access. On such questions as whether your doctor has early morning hours, evening availability, or weekend slots, we're not trailing the pack, but we're not in the lead, either. On evening hours, for instance, we lag behind Australia, Canada, Germany, and New Zealand. On same day appointments, Only 30 percent of Americans report that they can access a doctor on the very day they need one, as opposed to 41 percent of Britons and 55 percent of Germans. And a full 67 percent of Americans—more than in any other country—say it's difficult to get care on nights, weekends, or holidays with resorting to the emergency room, where care is costlier and, if your injury is not grievous, less efficient.

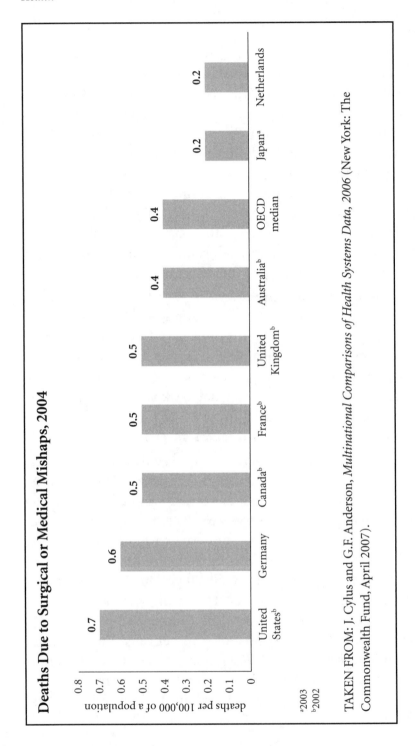

Deaths Due to Surgical or Medical Mishaps, 2004

deaths per 100,000 of a population

United States[b]	0.7
Germany	0.6
Canada[b]	0.5
France[b]	0.5
United Kingdom[b]	0.5
Australia[b]	0.4
OECD median	0.4
Japan[a]	0.2
Netherlands	0.2

[a]2003
[b]2002

TAKEN FROM: J. Cylus and G.F. Anderson, *Multinational Comparisons of Health Systems Data, 2006* (New York: The Commonwealth Fund, April 2007).

We Pay for No Superior Service

Our doctors don't listen to us. But maybe the amount we're paying comes in customer service—maybe our doctors spend more time with us, are more reassuring, are more attentive to our cases. After all, we basically like the care we get. Our overall self-evaluation of the treatment we receive is solidly in the middle of the pack, with 70 percent expressing satisfaction—which means we're less satisfied than the Canadians, Australians, and New Zealanders, but 5 percent above the Britons, and well above the Germans or Dutch. But when you ask for specifics, we do a bit worse.

Americans are the least likely to report that their doctors explain things in ways they understand (though the spread on this question is rather small) or say doctors spend enough time with them (56 percent of us say they do, as compared to 70 percent of Germans). We're the most likely to report that test results or medical records were unavailable during our scheduled appointments and, along with the Germans, the most likely to say that our doctors ordered tests that we'd already had done. On the bright side, 78 percent of us say our regular doctor was "informed and up-to-date" about follow-up care after a hospital visit.

We have high rates of chronic conditions. Aside from the surprisingly unhealthy Australians, Americans have the highest rate of chronic disease. And this isn't only a comparative problem; our high rates of chronic disease are a massive cost-driver, attributable, according to the research of Ken Thorpe, for about $2/3$ the rise in health spending over the past few decades.

But we're not treating them properly. So given the high prevalence of such diseases, and the pressures they exert on our system, you'd hope our system had evolved so as to treat these diseases more effectively.

Not so. One of the big issues with chronic disease is coordination of care. Illnesses like diabetes and kidney failure have so many manifestations, and require so much maintenance, that it's critical for care providers to have a full picture of what treatments are being received, what the patient's medical history is, what therapies they will and will not follow, etc. And for that reason, it's critical for the patients to have a single medical home—a regular care center where their case is understood, tracked, and treated. Sadly, we're tied with the Canadians for the lowest percentage reporting a single "medical home."

Worse, we're far and away the likeliest to report spending more than $500 out-of-pocket on prescription drugs annually. That's a problem, as higher out-of-pocket costs mean more of us going without prescriptions, which means less maintenance of conditions and, thus, more cost when our chronic illnesses balloon into catastrophic health events. Indeed, 42 percent of Americans with chronic conditions—the exact same percentage who report paying more than $500 for drugs—report skipping care, drug doses, or doctor's appointments due to cost. That's cheaper for them in the short-term, as they can spend some of the money on food or rent. It's more expensive for us, however, as we pick up the huge bill when they end up in the hospital in full cardiac arrest.

Victims of the System

We're frequent victims of medical, medication, and lab errors. Along with Australians, Americans are the most likely to report a medical, medication, or lab error, with 20 percent saying they've experienced one of the above over the past year. For those of us with chronic diseases, the rates are even higher. There are many reasons for this, ranging from our low adoption rate of electronic medical records to our splintered care system. But the effects are bad for our health and, needless to say, bad for our insurance rates. Conservatives make a huge deal out of medical malpractice claims, but studies show that our high rate of lawsuits is due to our high rate of medical error. The crisis isn't just in the courtrooms, it's on the operating tables.

Most of us are dissatisfied with our current system. In health polling, happiness with the system is generally measured through a three-answer question: Does your system merely need minor changes, as it works pretty well? Does it need fundamental changes? Or does it need to be rebuilt? Of all the countries surveyed—including the supposedly dystopic U.K. and Canada—Americans are the least likely to report relative satisfaction, and the most likely to call for a fundamental rebuilding. Only 16 percent of us are happy. In Canada and the U.K., that number is 26 percent. In the Netherlands, it's 42 percent. Meanwhile, 34 percent of Americas want to completely rebuild. Only 12 percent of Canadians say the same, and only 15 percent of U.K. residents want a new system. So paying more than twice as much as anyone else, we have *the lowest* satisfaction with our health care system. Lower than the countries with waiting lines. Lower than Germany, and Australia, and New Zealand.

And perhaps this shouldn't be a surprise. Is it any wonder that Americans who have to forgo care are less satisfied than Canadians who simply have to wait for elective surgeries? That our shorter doctor visits, more impersonal caregivers, higher rates of medical errors, and inability to find primary care after 6 p.m. have left us frustrated? And that our sky-high costs have, finally, left us aching for change?

There is no other area of American life where we collectively accept such a bad deal. We spend . . . more than any other nation on our military, but our military is unquestionably the mightiest in the world. We spend the most on our universities, but our universities are the best on the planet. But we spend the most on our health care—twice as much as anyone else—and our health system is mediocre-to-poor, with 47 million of us lacking the insurance necessary to easily access it. It's not surprising that Americans want change.

"Incentives work, and competition works. . . . We need to . . . engage the power of consumers to transform our health sector to become more efficient, more responsive to consumer needs, and more affordable."

A Free-Market Approach to Health Care Will Keep Costs Down

Grace-Marie Turner

In the following viewpoint, Grace-Marie Turner argues that the American health care system must change, and that a consumer-driven market should be in the forefront, leading to more individual control, lower costs, and greater efficiency in the system. She asserts that choice and competition will provide incentives for consumers to keep their own health care costs low. She argues that President George W. Bush's health care plan, announced in January 2007 and involving significant tax deductions for health insurance, will provide a good solution to the health care debate. Turner is the president of the Galen Institute, a nonprofit research organization.

Grace-Marie Turner, "Toward Free-Market Health Care," *Heritage Lectures*, May 4, 2007. Copyright © 2007 The Heritage Foundation. Reproduced by permission.

As you read, consider the following questions:

1. How many Americans change jobs every year, according to the Labor Department?

2. What is one of Senator Ted Kennedy's top priorities, according to Turner?

3. What is the centerpiece of President Bush's plan, according to Turner?

Our health care sector must change to meet the challenges of a 21st-century economy. Consumers, not just in the United States but in all developed countries, are demanding a much greater role in decisions involving their health care.

People can find on the Internet a wealth of information about diseases, diagnoses, and treatment options, but all too often, they must fight bureaucracies and paperwork all along the way. Women especially believe that they, rather than a corporate human resources director, could make better decisions involving health coverage for their families if only they were given the chance.

In addition, many who have health insurance are worried that if they lose their jobs, they will lose their health insurance. And with the cost of health insurance and health care rising every year, they fear they would not be able to afford coverage on their own. The middle class is increasingly afraid that they are one premium payment away from joining the ranks of the uninsured.

The Need for Portable Health Insurance

Meanwhile, our system of tying health insurance to the workplace is becoming antiquated with a workforce that is increasingly independent and mobile. The Labor Department reports that four in ten Americans change jobs every year. With this kind of job mobility, it is extremely difficult to tie health insurance to the workplace and expect people to have continuity of coverage. People lose their jobs, and they lose their health insurance. We need a system that allows people to have health insurance that is portable; insurance that they can own and control; insurance that they, and not a politician or a human resources department, decide is right for them and their families.

This move toward more individual control over health care decisions and health care spending is part of the global movement toward health care consumerism. Giving people more power and control over their health care and health insurance creates new incentives for people to be more engaged in managing their health.

Many companies realize this and are instituting new programs to give employees incentives to better manage their health spending. And they are creating new programs for those with chronic illnesses, like diabetes and asthma, to be partners in managing their care. A number of studies have shown that if people are given the tools, the information, and the incentive to manage their care, outcomes can be dramatically improved.

America Is Leading the Way

America can lead the way in creating a health care system that fits with our 21st-century economy by putting in place new policies that allow innovation to continue and that is better able to respond to consumer demands and preferences. But public policy changes are needed to lead us in a new direction.

Our health sector is like a giant ship: It takes a great deal of effort to change direction, but even a small change can lead to a very different destination over time. For the past six years [from about 2001–2006], the health sector has been moving toward more free-market solutions, introducing patient choice and competition into a system that had been largely dominated by top-down, centralized management. A few very familiar examples:

1. Consumers have new incentives to become partners in managing their health costs through financing options like Health Savings Accounts and company-based Health Reimbursement Arrangements. Both individuals and companies are saving money on health costs as a result.

2. Choice and competition also have been introduced in public programs like Medicare and Medicaid, showing that people can choose among competing health plans that have new incentives to offer better benefits at lower costs.

Competition is working, but there are threats on the horizon. The new leadership in Congress is setting a clear agenda that involves expanding government health care programs and cutting back the initiatives begun over the past several years to bring more competition and patient choice into private and public programs.

Key committee chairmen want to expand government coverage of children, putting children in families earning up to $83,000 a year and "children" as old as age 25 into government-run plans. In addition, Senator Ted Kennedy has put as his top priority enacting legislation that would put all Americans on government-run health care through Medicare-for-All. Others are working to expand Medicaid to more middle-income Americans, shifting tens of tens of millions of Americans into government health care.

Innovative Solutions to the Health Care Dilemma

So what can we do?

The health care initiative that President [George W.] Bush offered during his State of the Union address in 2007 could usher in the changes that would continue to make the U.S. the leader in quality health care while addressing the growing problem of the uninsured and middle-class anxiety about high health costs.

The [former] President would give families the opportunity to own health insurance that is portable from job to job, and he would free up some of their tax money to help them buy the coverage. The White House estimates his plan also would give a tax cut to 100 million working Americans and provide health insurance to up to 9 million more Americans without any new long-term costs to the federal treasury. The dynamic changes in the marketplace for health insurance would transform the system to offer health insurance that is more affordable, flexible, and portable.

The centerpiece of Mr. Bush's plan is a new standard deduction for health insurance. It would be available to any taxpayer who buys qualifying health insurance. Families would get a new $15,000 standard tax deduction, and individuals would get $7,500. You need not itemize and will get the full deduction even if the policy you buy costs less as long as it meets certain minimum requirements for catastrophic coverage. Families earning $50,000 a year could save more than $4,300 in income and payroll taxes and use the tax savings to buy health insurance.

Benefits for the Uninsured and the Insured

What about the uninsured, especially those with lower incomes? The White House says the proposal would lower the average tax bill of a family without coverage by $3,350. This would mean $3,350 of their pay would be available to buy insurance instead of going to taxes.

But for many of the insured, this still would not be enough, so there is a second part to the President's plan involving the states: Health and Human Services Secretary Mike Leavitt (former governor of Utah) is meeting with every governor to find out what his or her state needs to create "Affordable Choices" in health insurance. Secretary Leavitt wants to help states make basic, affordable private health insurance policies available to their citizens. This could include, for ex-

Competition Is Good for the Health Care Market

Commentators have extensively analyzed the application of competition and antitrust law to health care. In general, these commentators have concluded that increased competition has empowered consumers, lowered prices, increased quality, and made health care more accessible. The [Department of Justice and the Federal Trade Commission] have long held that standard antitrust analysis and doctrines apply to health care markets. With rare exceptions, the antitrust laws are rules of general applicability, and they govern health care markets in largely the same way that they govern other markets. . . .

The optimal balance between competition and regulation is an enduring issue. Just over thirty years ago, the Senate Judiciary Committee, Subcommittee on Antitrust and Monopoly held six days of hearings on Competition in the Health Services Market. Senator Philip A. Hart opened the hearings with the following prescient observations:

> Over the years, health care service has been treated pretty much as a "natural monopoly." It has been assumed that a community could support only so many hospitals; that providers just naturally control supply and demand. And there may be validity to such ideas. But, in this area, as in many others which have long been thought of as "natural monopolies," today questions are being raised as to just how pervasive the monopolization must be. Isn't it just possible, some are asking, that turning competition loose, at least in some sections, may not only lower the costs of health care but improve its quality? . . .

David A. Hyman, et al.,
"Improving Health Care: A Dose of Competition,"
Department of Justice and the Federal Trade Commission,
July 2004, www.doj.gov.

ample, grants in the form of vouchers or refundable tax credits to help low-income people purchase private health insurance.

The President's proposal was very innovative and took the policy community by surprise with its boldness. The President described his basic philosophy to enthusiastic applause on both sides of the aisle during his State of the Union Address when he said, "in all we do, we must remember that the best healthcare decisions are made not by government and insurance companies, but by patients and their doctors."

Changing the Conversation about Health Policy

This changes the whole conversation in the health policy debate. No longer are we simply talking about how much or how little to expand government programs. We now can have a new national debate over how to engage the power of consumers in transforming our health sector to become more efficient, more responsive to their needs, and more affordable. In addressing the core problem of our current dysfunctional tax treatment of health insurance, the President has won support from the *Washington Post,* the *Wall Street Journal,* and experts from think tanks as traditionally divergent as the Urban Institute and The Heritage Foundation.

Does everyone like this? No, of course not. Congressional leaders have said the proposal is dead on arrival. It is such a new and creative idea that it will take time for people to analyze and digest the plan and its implications.

- Many are fearful that it will accelerate the decline of employment-based health insurance by giving a tax break to individuals who buy coverage on their own. But job-based coverage already is declining. This will give employers and employees a new negotiating tool to bargain for insurance that offers the best value.

- Others say it doesn't do enough for the uninsured and that tax credits rather than a tax deduction would be better. Using some of the "Affordable Choices" money, states can put new resources on the table to provide state-based tax credits, vouchers, or other new subsidies to the uninsured to supplement the federal tax break.

The Bottom Line

There are many more details than we can get into here and which will be addressed over time, but what's the bottom line? The President's plan is a win/win/win/win/win:

- It is a win for the uninsured because it offers millions more Americans the chance to buy health insurance with the tax savings they will receive from the new standard deduction and likely new state subsidies.

- It is a win for states because they will have more flexibility with the new "Affordable Choices" state initiative to direct federal resources to meet the needs of citizens to get affordable health insurance.

- It is a win for employees because they now have the opportunity to buy health insurance that they can own and take with them from job to job, and it gives them more control over decisions involving their health insurance and health care.

- The health sector wins because this eliminates one of the major hidden forces driving up the cost of health insurance and gives the market new incentives to make insurance more affordable.

- Taxpayers win because 80 percent of them will receive a tax cut when they take the new $15,000 family deduction.

Sharpening the Debate

This idea sharpens the debate between those who believe that the answer to the problems in the health sector lies in much more government involvement through expansion of public programs and those who believe that the free market can and does have much more potential to get health insurance costs down and provide people with greater access to coverage and more choices.

Incentives work, and competition works. What we need to do is engage the power of consumers to transform our health sector to become more efficient, more responsive to consumer needs, and more affordable.

"*The proposition that a so-called
private-market approach to health care
would be the best means of controlling
the cost and quality of care . . . does
not find empirical support.*"

A Free-Market Approach
to Health Care Will Not
Lower Health Care Costs

Uwe E. Reinhardt

In the following viewpoint, Uwe E. Reinhardt argues that Americans too frequently confuse the terms social insurance *and* socialized medicine. *Further, he asserts that social insurance has many advantages over private insurance health care in performing the functions expected of a health system. He also argues that free-market versus government is a false dichotomy. Lastly, the government has demonstrated that Medicare, a form of social insurance, is more cost effective than private health insurance. Therefore, he contends, the private-market health care arguments are not substantiated by the evidence. Reinhardt is a professor at Princeton University.*

As you read, consider the following questions:

1. What are some of the advantages Reinhardt lists for social insurance systems?
2. What are the five functions Reinhardt assigns to a health system?
3. How much more would a taxpayer be required to pay using a private Medicare Advantage program over a traditional, government-run Medicare program?

As the presidential campaign goes into full swing [in the fall of 2008], the American public is likely to be bombarded with the kind of misleading clichés and false dichotomies that distort serious discussion of health care reform in this country. One of these false dichotomies is "private market versus government health care" or "private market versus socialized medicine." Both terms mislead because their users seem not to understand precisely what the terms mean or, if they do, use them mischievously. The term "socialized medicine" in particular conveys to some an objectionably "un-American" form of government: socialism.

A major problem with the term "private market" is that the term refers not to one single thing, but to a wide range of alternative mixtures in which a government interacts with private players in the health care sector. In fact, there hardly exists a private market in which the government does not play some role. Worse, the term frequently is misused as a synonym for "competition," which, when placed in opposition to "government," implies that government-sponsored care is not and cannot be competitive. Yet competitive health care already thrives in heavily government-controlled health systems, like Medicare. In Medicare and in the Canadian provincial health plans as well, private and public providers of health care compete purely on quality of service for patients covered by government-run health insurance systems.

Finally, in the American vernacular the term "socialized medicine," when it is not being confused with "socialism" outright, often is confused with "social health insurance." But . . . these terms refer to very different things.

Distinguishing Social Insurance from Socialized Medicine

With "social insurance" a government operates or tightly regulates large risk pools to which individuals can shift the financial risks they face as individuals with premiums based on their ability to pay. Both Medicare and the Canadian government-run health plans work in this way. Typically, the sickest patients are not kept out of the pool, which includes all those who are eligible. Social insurance systems typically buy health care from a mixture of private for-profit and not-for-profit institutions. This takes place under both Medicare and Medicaid in the United States, under the single-payer, government-run provincial health plans in Canada and under Taiwan's government-run, single-payer health insurance system. Examples of social insurance outside of health care can be seen in the principle of limited liability for corporate shareholders, which has made modern capitalism possible, in the federal government's current [2008] bailout of Wall Street or in the federal government's provision of disaster relief to afflicted states.

By contrast, "socialized medicine" implies that a government not only organizes the risk pools for health insurance, but also owns and operates the health-care delivery system. The National Health Service of the United Kingdom or the county-based health systems of the Scandinavian countries represent socialized medicine, as does the health system of the U.S. Department of Veterans Affairs [V.A.]. Luckily for our veterans, the V.A. is now widely regarded as being on the cutting edge of the smart use of health-information technology and quality control. A European must find it amusing to hear

American politicians rant against socialized medicine while at the same time supporting the V.A. health system.

The Advantages of Social Insurance Systems

The advantages many proponents see in social insurance systems are these. First, they offer individual's financial protection over their entire lifespan. Second, they are relatively inexpensive to administer. Third, they obey the principle of solidarity, which requires that all members of society have access to needed health care on roughly equal terms. That principle is sacred in European nations, being viewed as part of the cement that forges a nation out of a group of people who happen to share a geography. It is a term not usually employed in the American debate on health policy. A pitfall inherent in these social insurance systems is that governments may underfund them.

In the United States, when private insurance is procured by an employer in the group market for health insurance, premiums tend to be community-rated over all the employees in the firm. In a sense, such group insurance may be described as private social insurance. Because that form of coverage is tied to a particular job, however, it is temporary and lost with the job. On the other hand, if private insurance is purchased by individuals in the non-group market, premiums tend to be "medically underwritten," which means that they reflect the individuals state of health. Such insurance, like the social insurance systems just described, usually does not provide coverage for the full life-cycle.

The Functions a Modern Health System Must Perform

To think more clearly about the issue of private market versus government care, it is helpful to list the distinct economic functions any modern health system must perform, and then to ask who best can perform each of those functions, given the ethical constraints a nation is willing to impose on its health system. The five functions are:

- the financing of health insurance and health care, by which is meant the process by which money is extracted (premiums or taxes) from households and individuals, the ultimate payers for all health care;

- the protection of individuals from the financial inroads of illness through larger risk pools (i.e., health insurance);

- the production of health-care goods and services;

- the prudent purchasing of these goods and services by or on behalf of "consumers" (formerly called patients);

- the stewardship of the health system, by which is meant the regulation of the health system to assure safety, quality, integrity and fair play among the various agents interacting in the health system.

Whether individuals, government, a nongovernmental entity or the patient best performs each of these functions depends on two distinct considerations.

First, ideally there should be a political consensus on the ethical precepts that the health system is to observe. Should health care be available to all members of society on roughly equal terms, or is it ethically acceptable to allow access to health care, its quantity and its quality to vary by income class? Should health care transactions be ruled by the principle of caveat emptor, or would that be unfair? Is it ethically acceptable, as it seems to be currently in the United States, to let individuals and households slide into bankruptcy because of unpaid medical bills? In their debates on health policy, Canadians, Europeans and Asians usually make explicit these ethical precepts and view them as binding constraints on public health policy. In the United States, remarkably, the social ethics of health care are rarely discussed explicitly. Instead, the ethical norms are allowed to fall out of the technical parameters—e.g., deductibles, coinsurance or the basis for setting insurance premiums—settled on in these debates.

Second, given an agreement on the social ethics that a health system is to observe, one can next inquire through robust empirical research who best performs each of the basic functions of health care: government, private not-for-profit entities, private for-profit entities or all of these.

Imagining a Laissez-Faire Health Care Market

To explore these two considerations further, it is useful to imagine initially a purely laissez-faire private health care market. In this context laissez faire means "let the health system do without government interference of any sort." For all of the advantages one may claim for such a system (for example, the unleashing of human ingenuity and entrepreneurial energy), the arrangement also would have a number of attributes many Americans might find dubious:

- Real resources in such a system would be allocated strictly to those individuals willing and able to bid the highest prices for them—that is, to the wealthier members of society.

- Individuals with superior information about the health care being sold in this market (e.g., physicians) would be able to take advantage of individuals with less information (e.g., patients).

- Individuals with superior mental acuity (the quick-witted) would be able to take advantage of the less quick-witted.

- In the short run at least, and possibly even over the longer run, individuals with more "flexible" moral standards would be able to take advantage of individuals with more principled moral standards.

It is clear that no modern society would long tolerate the unfettered operation of such a laissez-faire market in health care. Indeed, since the Great Depression no society has tolerated such a market even for much less complicated goods and services, like financial services. Recently, for example, the chairman of the Federal Reserve and the U.S. secretary of the treasury both realized that as simple a market transaction as a mortgage loan requires much stricter government control than that imposed on it in the years just before the subprime mortgage crisis.

A False Dichotomy

In sum, the choice in modern economies is never between government and private markets, but is among varying mixtures of government- and private-market activities. The false dichotomy between government and private markets is meaningless. Any politician caught mouthing that empty slogan should be asked to define precisely what is meant by those terms.

Medicare Is More Cost-Effective Than Private Insurance

But what about costs? It seems to be taken as an axiom in the U.S. debate on health care reform that private-sector institutions are inherently more efficient than are similar public-sector institutions, so that health systems relying heavily on private institutions operating in a free-market environment could control both quality and cost better than similar government-run institutions. That proposition, however, lacks any robust empirical foundation. In fact, the available research on this issue does not permit a general statement on the relative efficiency of different types of health systems.

To illustrate, it is frequently alleged that costs under the government-run Medicare program for the elderly are out of control, and that Medicare can be fiscally sustained in the fu-

Is National Health Insurance "Socialized Medicine"?

No. Socialized medicine is a system in which doctors and hospitals work for and draw salaries from the government. Doctors in the Veterans Administration and the Armed Services are paid this way. The health systems in Great Britain and Spain are other examples. But in most European countries, Canada, Australia, and Japan they have socialized health insurance, not socialized medicine. The government pays for care that is delivered in the private (mostly not-for-profit) sector. This is similar to how Medicare works in this country. Doctors are in private practice and are paid on a fee-for-service basis from government funds. The government does not own or manage medical practices or hospitals.

The term socialized medicine is often used to conjure up images of government bureaucratic interference in medical care. That does not describe what happens in countries with national health insurance where doctors and patients often have more clinical freedom than in the U.S., where bureaucrats attempt to direct care.

Single Payer FAQ,
Physicians for a National Health Program, 2008,
www.pnhp.org.

ture only if it is privatized, that is, administered by private health plans. The Medicare Advantage option introduced as part of the Medicare Modernization Act of 2003 is a legislative expression of just that opinion.

Under the program, however, taxpayers are required to pay an estimated average of 12 percent more for a beneficiary using a private Medicare Advantage plan than that same beneficiary would have cost taxpayers in the traditional, government-run Medicare program. In some regions, especially rural regions, the overpayment to private health plans is closer to 20 percent relative to traditional Medicare. If private health plans are more efficient purchasers of health care than is traditional Medicare, why do the private plans need extra payments to compete with government-run Medicare for enrollees?

Research has shown that when analyzed over several decades, Medicare spending per enrollee, although higher in absolute dollars than health spending for younger individuals, has not grown as fast as has health spending for privately insured individuals. As Cristina Bocutti and Marilyn Moon recently concluded in their comparative analysis of cost trends in Medicare and the private insurance sector: "Medicare has proved to be more successful than private insurance has been in controlling the growth rate of health care spending per enrollee. Moreover, recent survey research has found that Medicare beneficiaries are generally more satisfied with their health care than are privately insured people under age sixty-five."

Finally, it is well documented that in nations using social insurance, coupled with a mixed delivery system or outright socialized medicine, health spending per capita tends to be only about half of what is spent in America in terms of comparable purchasing power. Although some costly high-tech services in those countries are rationed by the queue, recent cross-national research funded by the Commonwealth Fund does not support the notion that the United States ranks among nations uniformly at the top in terms of health status indicators or quality indicators.

In short, the proposition that a so-called private-market approach to health care would be the best means of controlling the cost and quality of care, or the annual growth in health care spending, does not find empirical support.

Periodical Bibliography

The following articles have been selected to supplement the diverse views presented in this chapter.

John Abramson "Diagnosis for Health Care Is Bleak," *Albany Times Union*, November 12, 2006.

Carlos Angrisano et al. "Accounting for the Cost of Health Care in the United States," McKinsey Global Institute, January 2007, www.mckinsey.com.

Yaron Brook "The Right Vision of Health Care," *Forbes*, January 8, 2008, www.forbes.com.

Congressional Budget Office "Technological Change and the Growth of Health Care Spending," January 2008, www.cbo.gov.

Carmen DeNavas-Wait, Bernadette D. Proctor, and Jessica C. Smith "Income, Poverty, and Health Insurance Coverage in the United States: 2007," U.S. Census Bureau, August 2008, www.census.gov.

Micah Hartman et al. "U.S. Health Spending by Age, Selected Years through 2004," *Health Affairs*, Vol. 27, No. 1, January 2008, http://content.healthaffairs.org.

John McCain "Better Care at Lower Cost for Every American," *Contingencies*, September/October 2008, www.contingencies.org.

Joe Messerli "Should the Government Provide Free Universal Health Care for All Americans?" *BalancedPolitics*, September 25, 2008, www.balancedpolitics.org.

Ron Paul "Lowering the Cost of Health Care," *LewRockwell.com*, August 23, 2006, www.lewrockwell.com.

For Further Discussion

Chapter 1

1. After reading the viewpoints in this chapter, can you identify additional serious risks to human health not covered in this chapter? What do you think are the greatest risks to human health? Why?

2. How do you think that climate change will affect the health of citizens of the United States?

3. How does gender affect the health risks of an individual? Are there some diseases that affect only men or only women? Do some diseases affect men and women differently?

Chapter 2

1. In addition to the behaviors noted in the viewpoints in this chapter, what additional human behaviors contribute to or damage health?

2. What do you think should be the response to what has been called the "obesity epidemic" in the United States? Should the government and schools be involved? What role does advertising play?

Chapter 3

1. What are some ways that new technologies and treatments have contributed to human health?

2. What are some of the consequences, both good and bad, of computerizing all health records? Why is the protection of privacy such an important issue for so many of the writers in this chapter?

3. Statins, osteoporosis drugs, and other new drugs have both benefits and side effects. How safe do you think a treatment should be before being available to the public?

Chapter 4

1. What are the positive and negative characteristics of the American health care system, according to the writers in this chapter?

2. What are the different forms a national health insurance could take, according to the viewpoints in this chapter? Do you believe that the United States government should institute a system of national health care to cover all citizens? Why or why not?

Organizations to Contact

The editors have compiled the following list of organizations concerned with the issues debated in this book. The descriptions are derived from materials provided by the organizations. All have publications or information available for interested readers. The list was compiled on the date of publication of the present volume; the information provided here may change. Be aware that many organizations take several weeks or longer to respond to inquiries, so allow as much time as possible.

American Public Health Association
800 I Street NW, Washington, DC   20001-3710
Phone: 202-777-APHA
Web site: www.apha.org

The American Public Health Association is a large and diverse organization of public health professionals who work to protect Americans from disease and health threats. The organization publishes two important journals, *American Journal of Public Health* and *The Nation's Health*. On the organizational Web site are the fact sheet, "What Is Public Health?" and links to news items and other public health sites.

Centers for Disease Control and Prevention (CDC)
1600 Clifton Road, Atlanta, GA   30333
Phone: 800-CDC-INFO
e-mail: cdcinfo@cdc.gov
Web site: www.cdc.gov

A division of the United States Department of Health and Human Services, the CDC is the nation's premier public health organization. The mission of the CDC is "to promote health and quality of life by preventing and controlling disease, injury, and disability." The CDC Web site provides a wealth of useful and understandable materials on the subject of infectious diseases, including fact sheets, publications, news articles, and statistics. Sample publications include *Emerging Infectious Diseases; Morbidity and Mortality Weekly Report;* and *Adolescent and School Health.*

Committee to Reduce Infection Deaths (RID)

Attn. Betsy McCaughey, New York, NY   10028
(212) 369-3329
Web site: www.hospitalinfection.org

RID is a non-profit educational campaign and advocacy group devoted to fighting the causes of hospital infections. The Web site includes information about MRSA, the state of hygiene in American hospitals, and a list of fifteen steps patients can take to reduce their risk for hospital-originated infections. Also listed on the site are links to other publications, a newsletter, and a blog. Educational materials can be ordered through the Web site.

National Coalition on Health Care

1120 G Street NW, Suite 810, Washington, DC   20005
Phone: 202-638-7151
e-mail: info@nchc.org
Web site: www.nchc.org

The National Coalition on Health Care is an advocacy organization committed to the need for comprehensive health care reform in the United States. The organization's Web site provides articles and full-text speeches about the state of health care. In addition, the group also offers important fact sheets such as "Health Insurance Coverage," among others, containing statistical information about who is insured and who is not.

National Foundation for Infectious Diseases (NFID)

4733 Bethesda Ave., Suite 750, Bethesda, MD   20814
Phone: (301) 656-0003
Web site: www.nfid.org

The National Foundation for Infectious Diseases is a non-profit organization whose mission is to educate the public and health care workers about the causes, treatment, and prevention of infectious diseases. The organization's Web site includes a media center, fact sheets, and publications as well as specific information on meningitis, pertussis, tetanus, diphtheria, influenza, pneumococcal bacteria, and shingles.

National Health Information Center (NHIC)
PO Box 1133, Washington, DC   20013-1133
Phone: 800-336-4797
e-mail: info@nhic
Web site: www.healthfinder.gov

The NHIC is a United States government organization devoted to providing reliable health information. The NHIC maintains the Healthfinder.gov Web site, a source that provides an extensive encyclopedia of over 1600 articles from trusted sources on health topics. In addition, the Web site also provides access to up-to-the-minute health news as well as offering tools for individuals to assess their own health.

National Institutes of Health (NIH)
9000 Rockville Pike, Baltimore, MD   20892
Phone: 301-496-4000
e-mail: NIHinfo@od.nih.gov
Web site: www.nih.gov

The NIH is the medical research agency of the United States. The NIH provides consumer health information as well as information about clinical trials on its Web site. In addition, the Web site features relevant news stories as well as both audio and video programming.

The National Patient Safety Foundation
132 MASS MoCA Way, North Adams, MA   01247
Phone: (413) 663-8900
e-mail: info@npsf.org
Web site: www.npsf.org

The National Patient Safety Foundation is a non-profit advocacy group dedicated to improving patient safety. Its Web site includes significant information on MRSA infections and prevention as well as publications, articles, and links to other sources of information concerning patients and infectious diseases.

PandemicFlu.gov
U.S. Department of Health and Human Services
Washington, DC   20201
Web site: www.pandemicflu.gov

The Department of Health and Human Services offers a large, up-to-date, Web site that provides one-stop access to all U.S. government information regarding avian and pandemic influenza. It includes sections on health and safety, global issues, articles on the economic impact of flu, a newsroom, and a glossary. This site is essential for people interested in bird flu and the likelihood of a future pandemic.

UV Foundation (UVF)
6620 Fletcher Lane, Mclean, VA   22101
Phone: 703-677-6885
e-mail: info@uvfoundation
Web site: www.uvfoundation.com

The UV Foundation is an advocacy and research organization dedicated to "exploring the positive effects of UV light and to increasing public awareness about those benefits," according to the group's Web site. The organization's Web site includes a list of frequently asked questions, quick links to information about vitamin D and bone health, and dietary supplement fact sheets, as well as news articles concerning vitamin D deficiency.

World Health Organization (WHO)
Avenue Appia 20, Geneva 27   1211
   Switzerland
Phone: 41-22-791-21-11

e-mail: info@who.int
Web site: www.who.int

The WHO is the directing and coordinating authority for health of the United Nations. As such, WHO is a global force in issues of health and disease. The WHO Web site includes multimedia presentations, fact sheets, news articles, publications, brochures, and statistics. An essential starting place for any student of infectious disease, the Web site also offers on-line books for download and information on ordering materials through the mail.

Bibliography of Books

Deirdre Barrett
Waistland: The (R)evolutionary Science Behind Our Weight and Fitness Crisis, New York: W.W. Norton, 2007.

Shannon Brownlee
Overtreated: Why Too Much Medicine Is Making Us Sicker and Poorer, New York: Bloomsbury, 2007.

Robert N. Butler
The Longevity Revolution: The Benefits and Challenges of Living a Long Life, New York: PublicAffairs, 2008.

Jonathan Cohn
Sick: The Untold Story of America's Health Care Crisis—and the People Who Pay the Price, New York: HarperCollins, 2007.

Devra Lee Davis
The Secret History of the War on Cancer, New York: Basic Books, 2007.

William Douglas
The Health Benefits of Tobacco: A Smoker's Paradox, Miami: Rhino Publishing, 2004.

Madelon Lubin Finkel
Truth, Lies, and Public Health: How We Are Affected When Science and Politics Collide, Westport, CT: Praeger, 2007.

Eric Finkelstein and Laurie Zuckerman
The Fattening of America: How the Economy Makes Us Fat, If It Matters, and What to Do about It, Hoboken, NJ: Wiley, 2008.

Kathryn H. Jacobsen — *Introduction to Global Health,* Sudbury, MA: Jones and Bartlett, 2008.

Ichiro Kawachi and Sarah P. Wamala — *Globalization and Health,* New York: Oxford University Press, 2007.

Kurt Link — *Understanding New, Resurgent, and Resistant Diseases: How Man and Globalization Create and Spread Illness,* Westport, CT: Praeger, 2007.

Martin S. Lipsky — *American Medical Association Guide to Preventing and Treating Heart Disease: Essential Information You and Your Family Need to Know About Having a Healthy Heart,* Hoboken, NJ: Wiley, 2008.

Courtney E. Martin — *Perfect Girls, Starving Daughters: The Frightening New Normalcy of Hating Your Body,* New York: Free Press, 2007.

Stephen John Morewitz and Mark L. Goldstein — *Aging and Chronic Disorders,* New York: Springer, 2007.

Pete Moore — *The Little Book of Pandemics: 50 of the World's Most Virulent Plagues and Infectious Diseases,* New York: Collins, 2007.

Arnold S. Relman — *A Second Opinion: Rescuing America's Healthcare: A Plan for Universal Coverage Serving Patients Over Profit,* New York: PublicAffairs, 2007.

Mary Robinson   *Global Health and Global Aging*, San Francisco: Jossey-Bass, 2007.

Marwan Noel Sabbagh   *The Alzheimer's Answer: Reduce Your Risk and Keep Your Brain Healthy*, Hoboken, NJ: Wiley, 2008.

J.K. Silver and Christopher Morin   *Understanding Fitness: How Exercise Fuels Health and Fights Disease*, Westport, CT: Praeger, 2008.

Frank Harold Stephenson   *DNA: How the Biotech Revolution Is Changing the Way We Fight Disease*, Amherst, NY: Prometheus Books, 2007.

Gary Taubes   *Good Calories, Bad Calories: Challenging the Conventional Wisdom on Diet, Weight Control and Disease*, New York: Knopf, 2007.

Jill Bolte Taylor   *My Stroke of Insight: A Brain Scientist's Personal Journey*, New York: Viking, 2008.

John A. Weigelt   *MRSA*, New York: Informa Healthcare, 2008.

Index

A

A Public Health Crisis Brews paper (Infectious Diseases Society), 56
Acinetobacter gram-negative bacteria, 56
Actonel (risedronate), 136
Adults
  arthritis, doctor-diagnosed, 45
  obesity in, 41, 42, 45, 69–76
  tobacco use, 42
"Affordable Choices" state initiative, 183
African Americans and cancer, 37–38
AIDS, 19, 157
Alaska natives, 158
Alcoholism, 19
Alendronate (Fosamax), 132, 136
Alzheimer's disease, 16
American Academy of Dermatology, 104
American Cancer Society, 34, 37, 50, 67
American Diabetes Association, 50
American Health Information Community, 153
American Heart Association (AHA)
  cardiology/physician survey, 47
  Statistics Committee, 39–43
  on therapeutic lifestyle changes, 50
American Hospital Association, 165
American Indians, 158

American Medical Association, 104, 157–158
Ano-genital cancer, 25
Anorexia athletica, 91
Antibiotic resistant bacteria, 51–58, 64, 113
  Enterobacter, 56
  Klebsiella pneumoniae, 51–57
  methicillin-resistant *Staphylococcus aureus*, 51, 55–56
  Pseudomonas, 56, 57
Antibiotic resistant bacteria/ infections, 59–64
Antiresorptive drugs, 131, 132
Archives of Internal Medicine, 15
Arthritis, 45, 46–47, 74
Arthritis Self-Help Course (Stanford University), 46–47
Asthma, 74
AstraZeneca (drug manufacturing company), 115, 117, 118
Atherosclerosis, 48
Australia, health care attitudes, 168–175

B

Baby boomers, 14–15, 16
Bacteria, antibiotic resistant, 51–56
Basham, Patrick, 77–82
Bengoa, Rafael, 24
Beth Israel Medical Center, 108
Bigelow, James H., 141–147
Bioelectrical impedance analysis (BIA), 49
Bisphosphonate drugs
  alternatives to, 139–140

dangers of, 136–139
for osteoporosis, 130–132
Bland, Jeffrey, 44–50
Blood pressure. *See* High blood
pressure
Blood pressure medication, 122
Bloodstream infections, 54
Blount's disease, 73
Bocutti, Cristina, 193
Body image and exercise, 91–92
Body mass index (BMI), 71, 77,
79, 82
Bone mineral density (BMD),
129–134, 136–137
Boniva (ibandronate), 136
Brain cancer, 67
Brain cells and statin medication,
124–125
Brain tumors, 67, 121
See also Kennedy, Ted
Breast cancer, 35, 133
Brennan, David, 117, 119
Brigham & Women's Hospital, 115
Brown, Gordon, 78
Bulimia, 91
Bush, George W., 160–167
attacks on privacy rights, 152–
153
commitments of government,
164–165
competing philosophies, 161–
162
discounted care, 166–167
health care strategy, 162–163
HIPAA privacy rule imple-
mentation, 149
HIT adoption encouragement,
151–153
transparency issues, 165–166
2007 health care initiative,
179–180

C

Calcitonin (hormone), 133
Calcium, 133
Calories, 87–88
Canada
government-run health plans,
187
health care attitudes, 168–175
Cancer, 19, 21–32, 33–38
in African Americans, 37–38
common/deadly forms, 31–32,
34, 35
connection with infection, 25,
28
diagnostic methods, 34–35
diet/nutrition and, 30
global perspectives,' 23–24
preventative actions, 23
risk from tobacco, 24–25
statin medication and, 122–
124
treatment, 34–37
types of, 25, 32, 34, 35, 67, 84,
133
vitamin D and, 100
Western lifestyle and, 29–30
World Cancer Report, 22–23
See also American Cancer Society
Cardiovascular disease (CVD),
39–43, 44–50
contributing factors, 40
death from, 39–43
economic factors, 43
information resources, 40–41
lifestyle change reduction of,
44–50
risk factors, 41–43
screening, 46
Carey, John, 114–119

CATCH (Child Adolescent Trial for Cardiovascular Health) prevention program, 82
Cell phones, 67–68
Census Bureau (U.S.), 15
Center for Cardiovascular Disease Prevention (Brigham & Women's Hospital), 116
Centers for Disease Control and Prevention (CDC), 46, 61, 62, 80–81, 84, 158
Centers for Medicare and Medicaid Services (CMS), 145–146
Certification Commission for Healthcare Information Technology, 153
Cervical cancer, 25
Children
    cell phone usage, 68
    MRSA deaths, 5
    obesity data/epidemic, 41, 45, 74, 77, 79–82
China, 19, 20
Cholesterol levels, 40, 42, 48, 70, 74, 85
    high density lipoprotein, 74, 87
    low density lipoprotein, 87, 115, 116, 117, 118, 124
    statin use, health risks, 120–124
    statin use, benefits, 114–119
    See also Cardiovascular disease; Diabetes; High density lipoprotein; Jupiter cholesterol medication study; Kennedy, Ted; Low density lipoprotein; Scandinavian Simvastatin Survival Study; Statin medication
Church, Tim, 35

Coenzyme Q10 (CoQ10), 124
Collaborative Writing Committee, 50
Colon cancer, 32, 34, 84
Colonoscopy/colorectal screening, 32, 35, 37
Columbia University Medical Center, 35
Commonwealth Fund survey data, 168–175, 193
"Competition in the Health Care Services Market" hearings, 181
Computerized Physician Order Entry systems, 143
Congress (U.S.)
    expansion of health care debate, 179, 182
    health care privacy debate, 151, 153, 154
    HIPAA enactment, 149–150
    Medicare modernization, 163, 164
Consumerism in health care, 177–184
Consumers Union of the United States, 102–109
Conte, Joseph, 62–63
Costs of disease, 43, 46–47, 49
    cardiovascular disease, 43, 46–47
    free-market approach, 176–184
    HIT investments, 142, 144–146, 152, 170
    Jupiter trial, 119
    obesity, 78, 82
    osteoporosis, 127, 138
    See also Bush, George W.; Hand washing; Health insurance
C-reactive protein, 119

Crestor (cholesterol lowering drug), 115, 117, 119
Crohn's disease, 28
Cumella, Edward J., 90–96
CVD. *See* Cardiovascular disease

D

Dartmouth Medical School, 107
Death, causes of
    Alzheimer's disease, 16
    cancer, 22, 24, 25–27, 28, 31, 33–38
    cardiovascular disease, 39–43
    Klebsiella pneumoniae bacteria, 54
    natural disasters, 19–20
    osteoporosis, 15–16
    stroke, 41
Decision Support Systems, 143
DeLeo, Vincent, 108
Depression, 75
Detection of cancer methods, 34–35
Diabetes, 40, 42, 45, 46, 48, 70, 75, 84
    See also Insulin resistance
Digital records (in U.S.), 151
Donelan, Susan, 61
Driving by older drivers, 16
Drug addiction, 19

E

Eating disorders, 91
Eckel, Robert, 47–48
Economics of disease. *See* Costs of disease
Electronic Medical Records, 143, 150
Energy balance, 87–88

Enterobacter gram-negative bacteria, 56
Estradiol, 132–133
Etidronate, 130
Ettinger, Bruce, 138
Exercise, 71, 76
    body image and, 91–92
    CVD and, 44, 45, 48, 67
    goal setting, 49
    health benefits, 83–89
    for osteoporosis, 139
Exercise addiction (EA), 90–96
    screening for, 92–93
    as threat to life, 96
    treatment, 93–96
Exercise bulimia, 91

F

Fast foods, 71
Fatigue (from obesity), 71
Fatty liver, 75
Federal Interagency Forum on Aging (report), 14
Federal Trade Commission (FTC), 104, 181
Feinman, Jane, 77–82
Flory, Matt, 34, 35
Flu pandemic (1918/U.S.), 40
Food and Drug Administration (FDA), 99, 100, 119, 138
Food-borne disease, 20
Foresight report (United Kingdom), 78
Fosamax (alendronate), 126, 136
Free-market health care approach
    costs, negatives, 185–193
    costs, positives, 176–184
Fugh-Berman, Adriane, 135–140

G

Gallstones, 74

Gastrointestinal tract (GIT) tissue damage, 28

Gastro-oesophageal reflux disease, 28

Genetics of obesity, 71

Germany, health care attitudes, 168–175

Giske, Christian, 57–58

Global cancer rates, 31–32

Global health care system comparisons, 168–175

Global obesity studies, 81

Global warming, 19

Goldmann, Don, 62

Government's role in health care, 145–156, 160–167

   See also Bush, George W.; Health Insurance Portability and Accountability Act; Medicaid; Medicare

Gram-negative/positive bacteria, 52

Groopman, Jerome, 51–56

H

Hallisy, Julia, 62

Hand washing, 60–61, 62

Hart, Philip A., 181

Harvard Medical Center, 157

Health and Human Services (HHS) Department (U.S.), 149, 152–153, 180

Health care system functions, 188–190

Health care workers

   hand washing/hygiene practices, 60–61

   recommendations for, 48–50

Health information technology (HIT), 141–147

   benefits, 144

   certification process, 146

   costs vs. savings, 144–145

   implementation obstacles, 145

   loss of privacy from, 148–154

   need for governmental intervention, 145–147

   patient privacy rights, 149–154

   RAND policy recommendations, 145–147

   savings potential, 142–144

   See also Computerized Physician Order Entry systems; Decision Support Systems; Electronic Medical Records

Health Information Technology Standards Panel, 153

Health insurance, 49, 158, 165

   need for portability, 177–178

   private vs. Medicare, 191–193

   single-payer, 187, 192

   See also Health Insurance Portability and Accountability Act

Health Insurance Portability and Accountability Act (HIPAA), 149, 152–153

Health savings accounts, 165, 179

Heart disease, 19, 39–43, 44–50, 48

   contributing factors, 40, 85

   death from, 39–43

   economic factors, 43

   inactivity, consequences of, 85

information resources, 40–41
risk factors, 39, 41–43, 85–87
vitamin D and, 100
See also Cardiovascular disease; Cholesterol levels; Hypertension
Helicobacter pylori (stomach cancer), 25, 28, 31
HELP (Health, Education, Labor, Pensions) committee (U.S.), 121
Hepatitis B virus (HBV), 25, 28
Hepatitis C virus (HBC), 25
The Heritage Foundation, 182
Herson, Jay, 16
High blood pressure
    death from, 40, 47
    defined, 74
    overweight and, 70, 74
    physical activity and, 84
    as risk factor, 42, 86–87
High density lipoprotein (HDL), 74, 87
Hillestad, Richard, 141–147
Hip fractures, 137
HIPAA (Health Insurance Portability and Accountability Act), 149, 152–153
Hormone replacement therapy (HRT), 132
Human papillomaviruses, 25
Hurricanes, 19
Hygiene practices, 54, 59, 60, 61–64
Hypertension, 40, 42, 47, 70, 74, 84, 86–87
    death from, 40, 47
    defined, 74
    overweight and, 70, 74
    physical activity and, 84
    as risk factor, 42, 86–87

I

Ibandronate (Boniva), 136
Indoor Tanning Association, 97–101
Infectious agents, 25
Infectious Diseases Society, 56
Inflammation, systemic (of human body), 116, 119
Institute of Medicine (IOM), 56
Insulin resistance, 45, 48, 75
Insurance. *See* Health insurance
International Agency for Research on Cancer (IARC), 23
International Obesity Task Force, 78

J

James, Philip, 78
Jernigan, John, 60
Johns Hopkins University School of Medicine, 106
Johnson, Alan, 78
Johnson, Lyndon Baines, 162–163
Joint problems (from obesity), 73
Journal of the American Academy of Dermatology, 106, 107–108
Journal of the American Medical Association, 80
Journal of the National Cancer Institute, 107
Jupiter cholesterol medication study, 115, 118, 119

K

Karolinska University Hospital, 57
Kennedy, Ted, 121–122, 125, 179
Kidney disease, 40, 46

Klebsiella pneumoniae bacteria, 51–58
  classification/ramifications, 52–53
  comorbid conditions, 54
  deaths from, 54
  initial outbreak in U.S., 53–54
Kleihues, Paul, 23, 28
Klein, Ezra, 168–175

L

Labovitz, Jonathan, 126–134
Laparoscopic surgery, 112
Laser technology, 112
LDL ("bad") cholesterol, 87
Leavitt, Mike, 180
Leech therapy, 112–113
Levy, Stuart, 56–57
Liao, James, 115, 117
Lifestyle
  cancer and, 29–30
  cardiovascular disease and, 44–50
Lipitor (cholesterol medication), 116–117, 123
Liver diseases, 25, 31, 53, 75
Lloyd-Jones, Donald, 41
Low density lipoprotein (LDL), 87, 115, 116, 117, 118, 124
Lung cancer, 31

M

Maggot therapy, 113
Malignant tumors. *See* Cancer
Marcotty, Josephine, 33–38
Massion, Charlea T., 135–140
Mayo Clinic, 157
Medicaid, 187

Medicare, 17, 145–146, 162, 187, 191–193
Medicare Advantage Option, 192–193
Medicare Modernization Act (2003), 192
Medline medical database, 137
Melanoma, 101
Men and coronary heart disease, 42
Menopause, 15–16, 129, 133, 138
Metabolic syndrome. *See* Insulin-resistance
Methicillin-resistant *Staphylococcus aureus* (MRSA), 51, 55–56
  hygiene practices, 61–64
  prevention of, 60
  role of hand washing, 60–61
MetLife (Insurance Company) wellness survey, 46
Mevacor (cholesterol medication), 123
Moellering, Robert, 55–56
Moon, Marilyn, 193
Mosquito-borne disease, 20
MRSA. See methicillin-resistant *Staphylococcus aureus*
Mt. Sinai Medical Center, 54

N

National Academy of Sciences, 56
National Coalition on Health Care (NCHC), 158–159
National Diet and Nutrition Survey (UK), 80
National Health Service (UK), 187
National Heart, Lung, and Blood Institute, 83–89

National Institutes of Health (NIH), 40–41, 81, 118
National Safety Council, 68
Natural disasters, 19
Netherlands, health care attitudes, 168–175
Neugut, Alfred, 35, 36
New Zealand, health care attitudes, 168–175
Nightingale, Florence, 63–64
North Shore–Long Island Jewish Health System, 62
Nutrition
    cancer and, 30, 32
    counseling, 46
    exercise with, 48
    obesity and, 71
    See also Coenzyme Q10; Vitamin D; Vitamin K

O

Obesity
    in adults, 41, 42, 45, 69–76
    in children, 41, 45, 74, 77, 79–82
    in children/teenagers, 41
    defined, 70
    epidemic, 70, 78, 80
    exaggerated risks of, 77–82
    exercise benefits, 83–89, 84
    health problems from, 71, 73–76
    politics of, 78
    reasons for, 71
    studies, 81
    weight loss benefits, 47
    See also Body mass index; Cholesterol levels; Diabetes; Hypertension
Ochs, Ridgely, 59–64

Older Americans Month, 15
Organ transplantation and statins, 124
Osteopenia, 136
Osteoporosis, 15–16, 126–134
    bone health recipe, 131
    bone weakness from, 136–137
    complication prevention, 133–134
    drug harmfulness, 135–140
    exercise for, 139
    HRT/SERMS treatment, 132–133
    menopause and, 15–16, 129, 138
    risk criteria, 127–129
    treatments, 126–134
    vibration training for, 134
    vitamin D treatment, 133, 139
    See also Antiresorptive drugs; Bisphosphonate drugs; Bone mineral density; Hip fractures; Transverse bone fractures
Ovarian cancer, 133
Overweight. *See* Obesity

P

PAP smear, 25
Patient privacy rights, 149–154
Peel, Deborah C., 148–154
Personal health information (PHI), 150
Physical activity. *See* Exercise
Polycystic ovary syndrome (PCOS), 75
Polyps (in the colon), 37
Postmenopausal osteoporosis, 133
Predt, Robert, 15
Privacy rights of patients, 149–154

Progestin, 132

Prostate cancer, 15

Prostate Cancer Foundation, 15

Pseudomonas gram-negative bacteria, 56, 57

Pseudotumor cerebri, 75

R

Raloxifene, 132

RAND research organization, 142–147

    See also Health information technology

Rectal cancer, 32

Reinhardt, Uwe E., 185–193

Rice, Louis, 58

Richard, Josephine, 33–38

Richards, Byron, 120–125

Ridker, Paul, 116, 117

Risedronate (Actonel), 136

Risk factors

    Alzheimer's disease, 16

    cancer, 21

    heart disease, 39, 40–43, 85–87

    indoor tanning, 104

    osteoporotic fractures, 127–128

    skin disease, 107

    stroke, 41

Roberts, Christian, 48

S

Salmon calcitonin, 133

San Diego State University, 108

Sayani, Shohreh, 126–134

Scandinavian Simvastatin Survival Study, 118

Science Daily (Web site), 68

Selective estrogen receptor modulators (SERMS), 129, 132–133

Senate Judiciary Committee (U.S.), 181

Senior Journal.com, 16

Sigmoidoscopy, 35

Simvastatin (cholesterol medication), 118

Single-payer health insurance, 187, 192

Skin cancer, 101, 102, 103, 104, 106, 107, 109

Sleep apnea, 74

Slipped capital femoral epiphyses (SCFE), 74

"Smart" technology, 151

Smoking cessation, 129

Social insurance, 187–188

Socialized medicine, 187–188

Squamous cell carcinoma, 28

St. Luke's-Roosevelt Medical Center, 108

Stanford University Arthritis Self-Help Course, 46–47

Statin medication

    brain cells and, 123, 124–125

    cancer and, 122–124

    CVD prevention, 114–119

    efficacy of, 118

    risks to health, 120–125

    See also Cholesterol levels; Jupiter cholesterol medication study; Kennedy, Ted; Scandinavian Simvastatin Survival Study

Stewart, Bernard W., 23

Stomach cancer (Helicobacter pylori), 25, 28, 31

Stony Brook University Medical Center, 61

Streptococcus gram-positive bacteria, 52
Stroke, 39–43, 84
Stroke Statistics Committee, 39–43
Substance abuse, 19
Sudden infant death syndrome (SIDS), 158
Sun exposure, 100–101
Sunshine vitamin. *See* Vitamin D

T

Tamoxifene, 132
Tanning, 97–101, 102–109
    age factors, 108–109
    false claims about, 104–106
    health benefits, 97–101
    indoor, 104, 106, 109
    sun-bed safety, 107–108
    by teenage girls, 103, 106
    Wake Forest University study, 105
    See also Melanoma; Skin cancer; Ultraviolet (UV) light; Vitamin D
Technology. *See* Electronic Medical Records; Health information technology
Teenagers
    obesity risks, 41, 70, 71, 73–75
    tanning data, 103, 106
    tobacco use, 40, 42
TeensHealth.org (Web site), 69–76
Therapeutic lifestyle changes (TLC), 46–47, 48, 49–50
Third Report of the National Cholesterol Education Program's Adult Treatment Panel (ATP III), 46
Tisch Hospital (New York University), 52–54

TLC (therapeutic lifestyle changes), 46–47, 48, 49–50
Tobacco use, 19
    cancer risk from, 24–25
    heart disease risks from, 42
    U.S. adult/teen data, 40, 42
Transverse bone fractures, 137
Treatment of cancer, 34–35
Tufts University School of Medicine, 56–57
Turner, Grace-Marie, 176–184
2008 Alzheimer's Disease Facts and Figures, 16

U

Ulcerative colitis, 28
Ultraviolet (UV) light, 97, 98, 104
    LTV radiation, 107, 109
    medicinal properties, 98–99
    melanoma and, 101
    UVA/UVB rays, 106–107
    See also Vitamin D
United Kingdom, 78
    health care attitudes, 168–175
    National Diet and Nutrition Survey, 80
    National Health Service, 187
United States
    "Affordable Choices" state initiative, 183
    Alzheimer's data, 16
    antibiotic-resistant disease, 53, 56
    baby boomers, 14–15, 16
    cancer death rates, 34
    CATCH prevention program, 82
    childhood obesity, 80
    digital records, 151
    free-market solutions, 176–184

health care system, negatives, 168–175
health care system, positives, 160–167
heart disease death rates, 40, 42, 43
HIPAA enactment, 149
lack of health care, 170–172
mosquito-borne disease, 20
natural disasters, 19
private vs. government health care, 186–187
social insurance vs. socialized medicine, 187–188
tanning salons, 103
vitamin D deficiency, 99–100
See also Bush, George W.; Congress (U.S.); Costs of disease; Government's role in health care
United States Census Bureau, 15
University of Washington School of Medicine, 107–108
Urban Institute, 182
Urinary infections, 54

V

Veterans Affairs (V.A.) Department (U.S.), 187
Vibration training (for osteoporosis), 134

Vitamin D, 97, 98, 124
deficiency, 99–101
health benefits, 98, 100
indoor tanning and, 109
melanoma and, 101
for osteoporosis, 133, 139
See also Ultraviolet (UV) light
Vitamin K, 130
Vytorin (cholesterol lowering drug), 115

W

Ward, Elizabeth, 37–38
Water-borne disease, 20
Weight-related issues. *See* Obesity
Wetherbee, Roger, 52, 53, 54
Wilkowske, Mark, 34
Women and coronary heart disease, 42
World Cancer Report, 22–23, 28
World Health Organization, 19, 21–32

Z

Zetia (cholesterol lowering drug), 115
Zocor (cholesterol medication), 123
Zoledronic acid (Zometa), 136
Zometa (zoledronic acid), 136